HOW TO WIN NEW (

For a complete list of Management Books 2000 titles,
visit our web-site on http://www.mb2000.com

Also by the same author:

Close Close Close
Selling – the Most Important Job in the World
101 Ways to Boost Your Performance
How to Double Your Profits Within the Year
How to Get the Best Out of Today's Salespeople
How to Sell Your Higher Price

HOW TO WIN NEW CUSTOMERS

John Fenton

2000

First published in 1998 by Management Books 2000 Ltd

This new edition published in 2002 by Management Books 2000 Ltd
Forge House, Limes Road
Kemble, Cirencester
Gloucestershire, GL7 6AD
tel: 01285 771441 fax: 01285 771055
E-mail: info@mb2000.com

Printed and bound in Great Britain by Digital Books Logistics of Peterborough

British Library Cataloguing in Publication Data is available

ISBN 1-85252-409-X

Contents

VISION STATEMENT by HRH The Duke of Edinburgh 10
Foreword 11
Author's Health Warning 13

**Chapter 1 – How to Find New Customers Before Your
Competitors Find Them** **15**
Detectives and Carrots 16
Method 1: Local Job Advertisements 19
Method 2: Internal Promotions 21
Method 3: PLC Annual Reports 21
Method 4: District Council Planning Registers 23
Method 5: End of Call Questions 25
The Five Card Trick – The Ultimate Referral Technique 28
Be an Entrepreneur 33
The Cocktail Party 33
Car Spotting 34
Early Risers 36
Minders! 38
The Star Prize 38

Chapter 2 – How to Make 'Cold Canvassing' Productive **43**
Business Cards with a Difference 47
Titles 51
Put Yourself in the Customer's Shoes 52
The Jekyll-and-Hyde Technique 55
Cold Canvassing by Telephone 56
Once in a Lifetime – Yorick from Warwick! 57

Chapter 3 – How to Stop Competitors Stealing Your Customers **61**
Complaints Handling 64
The Ostrich Complex 65
The Odds 66
Rumours 68
Taking Advantage 70

Chapter 4 How to Win Business From Your Competitors   73
The Purchasing Cycle Plan   75
Short-circuiting the Politics   78
Be Better By Being Different   80
Focusing the Mind   82
What Would You Do?   84
Two Kinds of People   85
Be Better By Being Thorough   87
Using Survey Checklists   92
Survey Checklist – Problem Solving   93
Survey Checklist – Competitors   93
Be Better By Being Faster   94
No Reason to Change   94
Be Better By Being Honest   96
Tactics for Beating the Bribers   97
Course One   99
Course Two   99
Plot and Counter-Plot   100
Big Mouth!   102

Chapter 5 How to Win in the Exhibition Arena   105
Why Are You Exhibiting?   107
The Exhibition Budget   109
The Stand   109
The Staff   110
Promotion   110
The 'Hilton' Rule   111
The Barriers   112
Signs and Colours   113
Models   114
No Telephones   114
Hospitality and Hospitality Suites   115
It Will Start – Whether You Are Ready Or Not!   117
What You Can Do and What You Can't Do   118
Don't Forget the Excitement   119
Manning the Stand   120
D-Day Minus 7   122

D-Day Minus 1 124
D-Day 125
D-Day Plus 1 129
D-Day Plus 2 131
Competitive Tactics Checklist 132
D-Day Plus 3 133

Chapter 6 How to Win in Retailing **135**
Price Cutting 136
Coffee Service 137
Invite Browsers 137
Smiles 138
Make It EASY To Pay 139
The New Recruits 140
Returns Anywhere 142
You Need Regulars 143
Position, Position, Position 143
Summing Up 145

Index 147

JOHN FENTON doesn't just write books. He is in great demand as a **MAKING IT HAPPEN** management consultant and trainer, as the testimonials on these two pages demonstrate:

"I was surprised what opportunities we as a Company were missing."
Timothy Jackson
Somers Handling Limited

"It really worked. This has been the best selling year in our history. New orders are more than 40% up on last year and success stories spread across every product line and every sales area."
Philip Bullus
Bournes Electronics Limited

"We have actually managed to increase our business over the past two years by 25% per year, a lot of which could not have been achieved had we not used the information and ideas given by you."
Dick Goodall
Aquatech Marketing Limited

"It gave us the answers to questions we didn't even know we should be asking - AND practical solutions to many other problems."
Richard Frost
Barpro Storage Systems

"Excellent, stimulating, practical, true, feasible, vital."
A. E. Judd
Industrial Division - Crane Heatex

"Mind Blowing."
Phil Cooper
Abbotts Packaging Limited

"Impressive and important. Can't fail to improve results."
Peter McArthur
Link 51

"Really worthwhile and absolutely worth every penny."
Vincent Brinkhof
Standard & Poor's

"So many simple ideas that can greatly increase our business."
Angus Beston
Protim Solignum Ltd

"Excellent. It has provided many new ideas."
Roger Chadwick
Labeltech Ltd

"Many managerial tips for steering our 'ship' through the stormy waters of this unending recession."
Brett Hacket
William Hacket Ltd

"Excellent. A great deal of food for thought, plus months of Action Plans."
David Broadbent
Northern Joinery Ltd

"VERY good. Refreshed old ideas and gave a valued injection of Fentonisms. All parts were relevant."
Alan Pearson
Thermon (UK) Ltd

"Excellent. It generated precise logical thinking in preparing a structured plan to increase business."
Mike Turness
Thomas Sanderson Blinds Ltd

"Thank you for an enlightening day of Action Planning."
Richard Leonard
British Industrial Sand Ltd

"I've come back brimming full of new plans for increasing sales - and re-charged personally."
Peter Yeats
Lilleshall Steels Ltd

To discuss what JOHN FENTON can do for your business, write, fax tel. or e-mail to John Fenton Stratagems Plc.

Clifford Hill Court, Clifford Chambers, Stratford upon Avon, CV37 8AA
Tel: 01789 266716 or 298739 Fax: 01789 266409 or 294442 E-mail: fenton@waverider.co.uk

---

"If you want to turn quotes into orders, you need to make these changes."
Magda Sargent
Guardsman Limited

"Identified shortcomings of existing quotation format. New and different approaches to increase conversion rate. Objectives fully achieved."
Graham McKenzie
Riverside Plastics Limited

"Thank you. Quoting has stopped my business committing commercial suicide."
Stuart Gizzi
Altecnic Limited

"Excellent. It made me step into my customer shoes."
Alan Squires
Flexiprint Limited

"Many new ideas on how to make the customer more aware and how to incorporate more of the essential information that we tend to take for granted."
Andy Hunt
Anti-static Technology Limited

"It made my thought process open out, especially on how to support a formal tender with valid and valuable material and improve the presentation."
Brian Burchell
Robinson Healthcare

"I learnt how to modularly produce quotations to suit my customers' needs instead of my own. It has inspired me to change possibly ALL aspects of how we quote."
Charlotte Foster
Computionics Limited

"Brought out many errors in current practice and will enable us to move from legal quotations to selling proposals."
A. E. Poeton
A T Poeton & Son Limited

"Our retained margin has in creased by 8%, our proposals to order ratio has halved, from 8 to 1 down to 4 to 1 and the number of testimonials increases daily."
Steve Wall
Gearhouse Ltd

"Your input on how we quote meant that we improved turnover by 20% on last year and maintained our margin."
Eddie Mander
CGS Catering Equipment

"Your CFO List has given us an edge not one of our 400 competitors can beat."
Ian Garner
The Hobart Manufacturing Co. Ltd

"Your proposal folder, testimonials and CFO List will give us another £10 million sales over the next three years, for the same number of quotations."
Chris Smith
Southern Print (Web Offset) Ltd

"So far, I've had 100% success closing proposals that I've produced since you gave us the know-how."
Martin Sewell
Marketing Initiatives Ltd

"Our Quotes to Order Ratio has improved from 25 to 1 down to 4.5 to 1 since you gave us the treatment. That's 5.5 times as many Orders from the same number of Quotations."
Ernie Johnson
GKN Sankey Limited

VISION STATEMENT

The Profession of Selling

It is a glaring glimpse of the obvious to say that no amount of production is the slightest value unless the products are sold for cash.

Selling is the very crux of any commercial or industrial enterprise.

It therefore stands to reason that, as a nation which depends so heavily on selling our products abroad, it is very much in the national interest that the highest standards and the most advanced techniques in salesmanship should be encouraged.

HRH Prince Philip

Duke of Edinburgh KG, KT

Foreword

Don't believe the Media

What credibility has the Media – newspapers, radio, television – which crucifies Selling at every opportunity, yet still refers to it often as 'The Second Oldest Profession'?

Note the word PROFESSION.

Okay, just like any other profession, including solicitors, accountants and bankers, there are and always will be those few bad eggs which the Media will be quick to headline. But notwithstanding this, let us not have any argument about it – Selling should be TOP of the league table of professions.

It IS top in America. Why it isn't in Great Britain and many other countries is more down to the Media than to all other reasons put together. And the Media has brainwashed the education establishment to the extent that our schools actively discourage pupils away from any serious thought of a career in Selling.

In the Vision Statement to this book, HRH Prince Philip, the Duke of Edinburgh says:

"Selling is the very crux of any commercial or industrial enterprise."

Positive, dynamic, enthusiastic Selling can do more to boost the economy and increase employment than anything else. And do it faster than anything else. In all walks of life, Selling is as essential as food and drink.

Customers don't beat a path to many doors these days. Only when someone develops something extraordinarily better or half the price of what went before. Everywhere else the inertia of human nature (bone idleness) causes the minimum to be purchased – unless sales promotion stimulates interest and salespeople convert that interest into orders.

11

In industry, if the salespeople at the 'sharp end' didn't sell, just about everybody in manufacturing and distributing would be out of a job. Same for the service industries.

In retail stores and at trade exhibitions, if customers were just left to browse and salespeople didn't try to positively create a specific interest and help those browsers decide to buy, very little actual business would happen.

Author's Health Warning

SELLING IS THE MOST EXCITING THING YOU CAN DO WITH YOUR CLOTHES ON

'There's new business out there, no matter how depressed the market.'

'All we've got to do is find it – and find it first.'

Chapter 1

How to Find New Customers Before Your Competitors Find Them

There *is* new business out there.

Not as much as in times of boom economy, but still some. It's more difficult to find, but it's *made* much *more* difficult than it should be by the salesperson's natural and **negative** feelings about actually looking for new business.

They don't like doing it!

In fact it would be true to say that the majority of salespeople only voluntarily look for new customers on warm, *sunny days. Never* in drizzle, ice or snow.

With this kind of attitude prevailing at the sharp end, is it any wonder that the growth potential of many businesses is so sadly under-developed? And looking for new customers – 'prospecting' – is so easy! Once you have developed a nose for it. You need to enjoy playing detective – that's all.

Detectives and Carrots

Good detectives succeed because they are inquisitive, because they employ method and because they have a purpose – to prevent crime and to catch criminals.

Good salespeople find new customers by being inquisitive, by employing method and with just as strong a purpose – to achieve and surpass target. To win more business than their competitors win.

The method couldn't be easier. All that has to be established is:

WHERE TO GO

WHO TO SEE

WHAT TO DO AND SAY

And from the knowledge they're building up, good salespeople know before they start the kind of people or the kind of business *most likely* to be prospects. So they know where to start looking.

They also know they have to be inquisitive enough to dig up what we call a **carrot** – a reason for making the first call.

That's what prospecting research is for – not just finding the 'suspect' and pin-pointing who the key decision-maker is – but digging up a carrot. This could be a problem the suspect is encountering, a project they're starting where your product or service might help, or a big contract they've just won. You have to look for something that will indicate the *possibility* that what you sell may be of use to them. Once you've found your carrot, the suspect becomes a prospect.

Once you have the carrot, you know what to say when you telephone for the first appointment. *And* you know what to say when you get face-to-face for the first time. Exactly the same words in both cases.

You've offered to discuss just the *possibility* that you might be of value to the prospect in one specific area – and that possibility seems reasonable enough for the prospect to say: 'Okay, I'll give you 10 minutes and see what you have to say.'

That is your **objective** – nothing more, nothing less.

You might find your carrot is no good after five minutes face-to-face. It may be quite clear that your 'possibility' area doesn't pan out after a few searching questions. No matter. By then you are asking questions in other directions and seeing quite clearly *other* possibilities and the best line to follow.

It *is sometimes* possible, of course, to succeed in winning a first interview *without* bothering to dig up a carrot to dangle – but it's certainly more difficult to win that way, and more risky. Why take the risk? All it does is increase your chances of failure!

That carrot you need can often be pin-pointed with just a phone call to someone in a suspect's business, other than the person to whom you will subsequently want to sell.

The phone call goes something like this:

'I wonder if you can help me? I sell widgets. I'm hoping to sell some to your company, but I'm short of a bit of information. If I can bend your ear for two minutes – what I need to know is – what sort of widgets do you use?'

(Answer – LISTEN)

'Where do you buy them from?'

(Answer – LISTEN)

'Who do I need to talk to – the person who buys or specifies your widgets?'

(Answer – LISTEN)

'Do you know if there are any problems on widgets?'

(Answer – LISTEN))

'Is there anyone other than Mr- that I should talk to about this?'

(Answer – LISTEN)

'That's super. Thank you very much. Goodbye.'

In a buyer's market, you should be looking for businesses that are doing well, expanding, and taking on people.

Detectives can do it ...

If you want to find new customers before your competitors find them – you've simply got to be a better detective than your competitors' salespeople are.

Here are five methods of finding these kinds of new customers.

Method 1: Local Job Advertisements

Consider the incredible amount of detailed information local job advertisements contain: what the company is doing; what equipment it has; why it wants the people for whom it is advertising; and, most importantly, the key contacts.

Here are a few lines from advertisements I've found in my own local newspapers:

'...is entering a phase of planned expansion which will double manufacturing capacity.'

'The successful applicant will be responsible to the Cash and Carry Depot manager for the total floor operation.'

'An important secretarial appointment. Secretary to the Chief Engineer. The job will include the supervision of the department's secretarial throughput.'

'For varied and interesting work in our new factory.'

Did *you* know they were building a new factory? How much of that doubled manufacturing capacity gives you scope for selling? What kind of things will that chief engineer's secretary be buying in a couple of months' time? It's all there – in these kinds of advertisements.

As a rule of thumb, if any company is advertising for more than one person, assume expansion.

If there's a box number for replies, so you can't tell which company it is, apply for the job. Send a very short letter from your home address: 'Reference your advertisement, please send me an application form'. They'll write back: 'Haven't got an application form, please send your CV', or they'll send you an application form. Either way you've got what you wanted – their letterhead, including the names of directors. Now you can telephone.

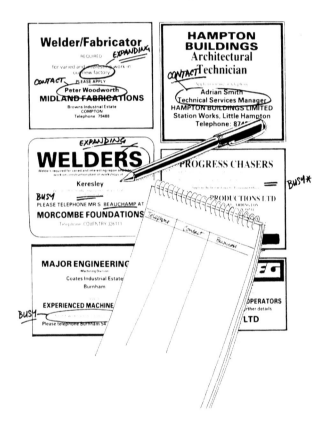

The most important job advertisements are those advertising for the key decision-makers themselves – directors, senior managers, purchasing managers and buyers. For these kinds of advertisements, you need a card index filing system. You give each advertisement a card, maybe sellotape the advertisement to the back of the card. The cards are filed in date order.

Four weeks or so *after* the advertisement appears in the local newspaper, you refer to the card and telephone the company that was advertising, to establish the name of the person who got the job. If you find you are too early, the card goes back into the filing system until you get the timing right. If the successful applicant has started the new job, you get his or her name – then you can either telephone or write.

Whichever you choose to do, you begin: 'Congratulations on your new job'. After that, it's easy. You're starting clean, and so is he. He's new and will want to make changes – to make his mark fast. And you may have been wanting to see changes in that company for years!

Method 2: Internal Promotions

Okay, in times of recession, there are fewer local job advertisements than in boom times. But this is compensated for by an increase in the number of internal promotions that businesses make. Maybe they have downsized. Or they cannot pay the necessary increases in salaries, so some people decide to leave. This is not necessarily indicative of a business that is coming out of recession, but it still gives you opportunities to get in and sell, so it is of key importance. Whatever the reason, someone gets promoted, and his or her picture, plus appropriate editorial, gets into the local newspaper.

Your plan of action is just the same as for the job advertisements, except this time you don't need the card index system. This time you can telephone or write straight away to the promoted person, beginning: 'Congratulations on your promotion'. The rest should follow. Why? BECAUSE VERY FEW SALESPEOLE DO THIS!

Method 3: PLC Annual Reports

Every Public Limited Company (PLC) whose shares are quoted on the Stock Exchange publishes an Annual Report to its shareholders. These Annual Reports contain an incredible amount of useful information, which helps you sell. Draw up a list of those PLCs you are interested in – existing customers as well as prospects – establish the date of their financial year end and, at the appropriate time (about a month after the end of their financial year), write to the Company Secretary at the registered office of the PLC and ask for a copy of the Annual Report. Make it a personal letter, not one from your company. You'll get the Report by return, plus a lot of other bumph. The Company Secretary has to assume you are a prospective shareholder.

Alternatively, use the free-of-charge service offered by the Financial Times, but this will be slower.

Apart from the balance sheet and accounts (which you *must* learn how to interpret, because these tell you how much money has been put aside for development and expansion or modernization), a PLC's Annual Report will contain the Chairman's statement. This can be your most valuable selling tool. Let me quote from a few Chairmen's

Statements to show you why:

'Obviously a setback of £5m off our profit budget is a very big handicap but we have decided none the less to go flat out for our original budgets. Despite this financial penalty, and to demonstrate our confidence in the future, we plan to invest approximately £230m in total over the next three years in public houses, catering and production facilities.'

'Plans for the modernisation of the ... division, including a move to a new single-storey building where production, warehousing and office functions will be integrated, are well advanced.'

'Operations by ... in handicraft kits and rug-making accessories have now been discontinued and the premises used for this purpose are being converted to more profitable use by the group.'

'We will not allow short-term cyclical movements in the economy to influence unduly out long-term strategic thinking. We have substantial unused financial facilities and will continue to implement our planned programme of expansion.'

There is your **carrot**, dug up and on a plate. And just imagine being face-to-face with an executive of the PLC with 'substantial unused financial facilities' with his Chairman's statement in your briefcase, hearing the executive saying to you 'We can't afford it'.

'What?' you'll say, showing surprise and pulling the Annual Report out of your bag. 'But your Chairman says here ...'

It's truly incredible how much you can broaden the discussions you have with PLC customers, just from what you learn about their businesses by reading their Annual Reports.

Remember, Confidence comes from Knowledge.

Method 4: District Council Planning Registers

Every application for planning permission to build something, or extend something, or change the use of a building, must, by law, be entered in the appropriate District Council's Planning Register.

There are 400 such Registers in the UK, and they are all open for inspection by the general public (that's you!) during normal business hours.

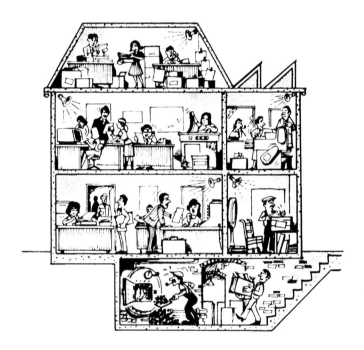

You'll get everything you need in the Register – developer, user, client, architect, contractor, project, surveyor, and the Council's decision.

You may not be concerned about buildings and building services – but you *will* be concerned about what goes on in, and around, the project when it is finished – be it boilers, toilet rolls, copiers, computers, cars, insurance, fire extinguishers, vending machines, paper, packaging, or whatever.

This is **advance** prospecting, and well worth the time of getting yourself down to every Council Office in your area once every month to find out what's in the register – before your competitors get there. If you want to WIN, that is! Better than that – attend the Council Meetings.

Method 5: End of Call Questions

More commonly called 'referrals'.

How many calls do you make in a year? 1000? 1500? 2000?

However many, on every single one of these calls you make there is the opportunity, at the end or somewhere during the call, to ask: 'By the way, do you know of anyone else who might be able to use our kind of equipment?'

Or, for retailers: 'I know things are pretty competitive in your business, but do you know of anyone else who it would be worth me calling on while I'm in this area?'

And for large companies: 'While I'm here, do you know of any other departments who might be able to use our services?'

And on regular, repeat calls: 'I know I ask you this every week, Charlie, but anyone worth me calling on, this time round?'

Ask the question religiously, every call (it doesn't matter what *kind* of call it is, *or* the status of the person you're asking) and some of your regular customers will begin feeding you names *before you ask*.

And whenever you get a name – even if it is one of your own customers – you don't stop, you keep on going with *more* questions. Chances are, your contact will know a lot more than you do about people and businesses in his own locale.

> 'What do they do?'
> 'What kind of widgets do they use?'
> 'Where do they buy them from?'
> 'Do they have any problem?'

Keep digging for those carrots. Give anyone an opportunity to talk about *someone else's* problems (they'll keep quiet about their own!) and the roof will blow off. You'll have trouble keeping up. It's the National Sport!

You probe for contacts:

'Who's your opposite number over there?'

or:

'Do you know the name of their chief buyer?'

and for friendships, or the opposite:

'Do you know him well?'

and you finish with:

'Well, thanks. Do you mind if I mention your name when I ring for an appointment?'

But if you're really good and he obviously knows well the person he's been talking about – you finish like this:

'I wonder, would you mind giving him a ring for me while I'm here – to see if he could see me today, while I'm in the area?'

Oh yes, they *will* do it. More than 60 per cent of them will do it. If you don't believe me, try it for yourself and see. But before you can try that finish, you've got to remember to start the ball rolling – to ask the *first* question. The incredible thing about salespeople is that most of them *don't remember* to ask the first question. They simply throw away probably 500 opportunities to get face-to-face with new prospects every year (if you make 1,600 calls a year, that's a 1 in 3 ratio of positive results from asking the question, batting average for most people who *do* remember).

One sales director I know got so annoyed with his salespeople forgetting something this good – and this basic – he fitted their briefcases with special handles which had engraved in them the words: **'ask the question'**. When they picked up their briefcases to leave the customer, they had to see those words. And I bet a few of his salespeople looked down at the words and said to themselves: 'What question?'

I tailor-made this referral technique not long ago to fit a small company that sells showers, door to door. The company had a team of five young lady canvassers and some installers. The canvassers weren't very good at canvassing, but they *were* good at getting orders – they were closing on average 20 orders a week total.

Only advertising and direct mail were generating new business enquiries, but this the company's managing director considered to be far too expensive.

'How do I get my team of young lady canvassers to use referral techniques?' was the problem he posed to me. 'Maybe you don't need to', I replied. 'What do you want to see your sales increase to?'

'I'd be happy with 50 orders a week', he told me. 'After that, I'll have problems with installation and delivery.'

'Okay', said I, 'forget your canvassers. You do it. Are you prepared to make 20 calls a week yourself, on the customers who had your showers installed, say two or three weeks ago? – and in the evenings?'

'No problem,' he replied.

'Right,' said I, 'just knock on their doors in the evening, out of the blue, no appointment, hand whoever opens the door your business card, introduce yourself and tell them you've just popped round to make sure everything is okay with the shower (and hope that everything *is* okay!)'.

'They'll be so surprised, and delighted, they'll invite you in for a cup of tea. They'll even turn off the TV. (Only managing directors have that much charisma!) And when they've finished telling you how nice the shower is, you say:

"Before I go, I wonder if you'd be kind enough to give *me* a bit of help. My job is to find people like you for my girls to talk to (not sell to) about showers. You're happy with yours. Can you give me the names and addresses of anyone else you know who you feel might be just as happy as you if they had one?"

'And off you go. You should average three names and addresses per call. Your girls will crack 50 orders a week within a month of your starting to make *your* calls. And don't come back to me with your delivery and installation problems; that's not my field.'

It's that easy to create your own opportunities for successful Selling – to take positive action and win. So will you use these five methods for finding new customers? Will you adapt the End of Call Questions technique to work for you – as I adapted it for the shower company?

The Five Card Trick – The Ultimate Referral Technique

The word 'trick' should not be in the professional salesperson's vocabulary, but with such a title as 'The Five Card Trick', it is irresistible.

This is the ultimate Referral technique; developed by J. Douglas Edwards and used by many Million Dollar Round Table members to keep themselves well over their MDRT qualifying target. The technique is not, however, restricted for use only in financial services. It can be, and is, used very successfully in other kinds of direct selling and in selling to industry.

The Five Card Trick is more than a technique, it is a game – a game played between salesperson and customer. The customer's natural curiosity to find out what happens next helps to make the technique successful.

The objective? To walk away from a call with *five*, yes, *five*, new and fully researched prospects given you by the customer you have just called upon, and for whom firm appointments have already been made on your behalf *by the customer*. (That's why this technique is the ultimate! But it is not, repeat not, for the novice salesperson.)

The Five Card Trick is *only* used when the situation is right for it. The customer is happy with what the salesperson has done. The customer is relaxed and not in a hurry to get on with something else, and has a few minutes to spare after the business with the salesperson has been satisfactorily completed. If all these conditions are 'go', the salesperson says:

'Before I go, I wonder if you'd be kind enough to spend ten minutes giving me a hand with how I have to do my business?'

If the situation is really 'go', the customer's reply will be 'Sure. What do you want to know?' or something like that. The salesperson then takes out of his jacket pocket five blank cards, each about 15 x 10cm, and lays them out in a line on the desk in front of the customer. While he's doing this, he doesn't say a word.

Then he begins asking questions. The questions he asks are ones that he knows, from his knowledge of this customer, will be pertinent to the customer.

'You've lived/worked in this area for some years now, haven't you? Is there anyone else you can think of who also lives/works around here who, you feel, might benefit from our product/services the way you have/are going to?'

The salesperson is searching for names. When he gets one, he writes it down on one of the five cards. If he gets two or three names as a result of his question, he writes one name only on each of two or three cards. His target is five names, one on each of his five cards. He keeps asking questions until he has achieved this target. No more, no less. Stop at five – always.

'Are you a member of any trade association? Last time you attended a meeting of the association, was there anyone there who, you reckon, could benefit from this the way you're doing?'

'Do you play any sports – golf or tennis or anything? Last time you were down at the club, was there anyone there who, you feel, might be able to use this?'

'Has anyone you know gained promotion recently? Gone up in the world so that his/her requirements may have changed and so will give us an opportunity?'

Each of the questions is designed to get the customer thinking about a relatively *small* number of people. This achieves the best results. Few people will provide you with names if they are trying to find one person out of 100,000 packing the National Exhibition Centre (metaphorically speaking!).

When each of the five cards bears a name, the salesperson thanks the customer and moves to stage two:

'Have you got your telephone directory handy? Could we together dig out the addresses and the telephone numbers of these people, just to make sure I have the correct ones?'

'Sure. Why not?'

The request seems reasonable to the customer. After all, there are probably 50 Charlie Browns in the telephone book. And, by this time, the customer's natural curiosity will have taken hold. No way is he going to stop until he finds out what's going to happen to those five cards. So together, salesperson and customer dig out addresses and telephone numbers, which are written on each of the five cards.

This completed, the salesperson silently re-aligns the five cards into a neat line, studies them for a few seconds, and then asks:

'If you were me, which one of these five cards would you call on first? Which one do you think would be the best customer for me?'

After a few seconds rubbing his chin, the customer will select one of the cards. The salesperson ask:

'Why did you pick that one? What makes him better than the other four?'

And the customer explains why he chose that person as number one. The salesperson notes the relevant data on the card. One fully researched, fully qualified prospect. Then he continues:

'Which one would you see as second best?'
'Which one is third best?'
'Which one is fourth?'
'Which makes this one last? Why is he not as good as the other four?'

Five fully researched, fully qualified prospects, lying there in a row. Any salesperson who gets this far could be forgiven for feeling elated. But the hardest part is yet to come. Not hard in the sense of difficult, but hard meaning having the guts to *do it*.

The salesperson picks up the number one card, offers it to the customer and says:

> 'One last favour. Would you ring Mr ... for me, while I'm here, and ask him if he can spare the time to see me sometime during the next few days?'

You won't believe it until you try it yourself, but more than 60 per cent of customers who are asked to telephone that number one prospect *do it*. And they do it with enthusiasm. And of course they give the salesperson the best possible impartial plug when they are talking to the prospect – they can't do anything else.

> 'You've got to see this guy, Charlie. He's got something that must be just up your street. He's here with me now. Wants to know if you can fit him in for half an hour, tomorrow or the day after. Or this afternoon, if that's not too soon for you. What? Yes, I've bought some. They look great.'

Better than this, every customer who telephones that number one prospect will also go on and telephone the other four. The salesperson's only uncontrollable risk is that the prospect doesn't answer when the customer rings.

For the less than 40 per cent of customers who say 'I'd rather not' in reply to the first offered card and the request for them to telephone on the salesperson's behalf, the salesperson says:

> 'Okay. Do you mind if I mention your name when I ring for an appointment?'

100 per cent of customers who turn down the salesperson on his first request, say 'Yes, of course' to his second request. No one can say 'No' twice running in this technique. And that's why the *guts to do it properly* are necessary.

So the jackpot is five firm appointments made on your behalf by a satisfied customer. The consolation prize is five fully researched, fully qualified prospects and the okay to use the customer's name when *you* telephone for an appointment.

Not bad for 10 minutes sheer professional enjoyment? That's really Selling!

Be an Entrepreneur

Be different. Stand out from the crowd. Do things that the average salesperson wouldn't even think of doing. That's the way to sell successfully against competition. How different? Let's take a few examples for finding new customers.

Cocktail Party Prospecting

Clive Holmes began his sales career selling carpets off the back of a van, then he rose to become the acknowledged king of the British Life Insurance business – a life member of the Million Dollar Round Table (to get that accolade you have to make the million dollar target in 10 consecutive years) and founder president of the Life Insurance Association. A very high FLIA indeed.

Very early on in his life insurance career, he discovered that if you tell a stranger you sell life insurance, the stranger disappears, almost in a puff of smoke. He found this particularly so at cocktail parties, which he frequented avidly, knowing that in the life insurance business, if you run out of people to sell to, you're out of business.

So he perfected a subtle change in technique for his cocktail party prospecting which went like this:

STRANGER (G & T in hand). 'What do you do for a living?'
CLIVE. 'I buy life insurance.'
STRANGER (puzzled). 'What do you mean, you buy life insurance?'
CLIVE 'I buy life insurance for people at the lowest possible cost for the maximum possible benefits. Would you like me to buy you some?'

33

The **Question you need the answer to...**
What is *your* equivalent to 'I buy life insurance'?

Car Spotting
I've spent a fair amount of my time over the years, trying to get car salespeople to stop sitting on their bottoms in their showrooms, waiting for the world to beat a path to their doors. Taking the demonstration car round the area, knocking on people's front doors and saying, 'Let me take you for a ride?' would be better than that, but gives problems with female customers if you don't get the words right!

Really switched-on car salespeople, determined to beat their many local competitors, also have an eye for where their profit comes from. Two places: from the sales of their new and A1 guaranteed nearly-new cars, and from the sale of cars they take in part-exchange from their customers – most of these vehicles being passed on 'through the trade'.

They know that if they sit in their showrooms and wait for customers to come to them, they have absolutely no control over the kind of cars they have to take in part-exchange. If they refuse to accept a part-exchange, they lose a sale. If they offer a silly price, the same thing happens. Yet they know that some cars hold their value better than others and are easier to sell on. So they go out into their area – *looking for these kinds of cars.*

They go out armed with a bundle of specially designed letters, lists of the new and A1 guaranteed nearly-new cars they have for sale, plain manila envelopes and their confidential copy of Glass's Guide (the trade price book for car dealers). They find suitable cars parked all over their area.

They examine the exterior appearance and bodywork of a likely looking parked car. They check the tyres. They can even test the shock absorbers if they're careful, by pressing gently down on a couple of corners. They can see the interior of the car and they can normally tell whether the car is privately owned or a company car, by its contents. They are looking for 'privates', not company owned.

They can see the mileage on the speedometer and know the age of the car from the registration number. So they have everything they need to decide a conditional price for that car.

They fill in the details on one of their specially designed letters. It reads like this:

Hello,

Your car, registration number ... ... is worth a lot more than you probably think. If the mechanical condition is as good as the body condition and if the mileage (...) shown on the speedometer is genuine, we would offer you £... for your car in part-exchange for any of the new or A1 guaranteed cars you'll see on the attached stock list.

Why don't you and your family drop into our showroom this weekend and let us give you a demonstration drive. No obligation.

And hire-purchase facilities have never been easier to arrange.

We look forward to seeing you.'

The letter and stock list go into a manila envelope and the envelope goes on the windscreen, under the wiper blade. A good car-spotting salesperson should be able to find and 'process' about 30 profitable part-exchanges a day.

The owner of the car comes back to the vehicle, sees the envelope on the screen and thinks: 'Hell, I've got a parking ticket'; gets into the car, opens the envelope in high dudgeon and finds it is *not* a parking ticket. The mood switches instantly from anger to pleasure. Just right for impulse-buy decisions. Some of them are down at the showroom within the hour.

Maximum prospects, maximum sales, maximum profit. Yet you don't see many car salespeople doing it, do you? Most of them are too busy thinking up reasons for not doing it!

Early Risers

It's the early bird that catches the worm! Never as true as in selling against competition. The entrepreneurial fork-lift truck salesperson, for example, got up very early a couple of times a month in order to be down at the local rail company goods depot before 8.00 am, while the van drivers were still sorting parcels and loading vans.

He was armed with a couple of packets of cigarettes and his A4-size survey pad (you can't sell successfully with anything smaller). At 8.00 am in the morning he had no trouble persuading half a dozen van drivers to stop work for a few minutes and join him for a fag.

'Please can you give me a bit of help?' he asked them. 'I sell fork-lift trucks in this area. Most of my trucks are used by companies for loading and unloading vans like yours. Do you know of any companies that you deliver to and collect from that don't have a decent truck, or don't have anything at all to help you load and unload the heavy stuff?'

Wow! Free fags and an opportunity to have a free moan at someone else's expense. The national sport again. The survey pad is full in minutes. A salesperson who does this kind of thing regularly will find such people waiting for him to come back, with their own lists of prospects for him. Some will ask for a sales brochure to give to one of the companies they deliver to, and will do some selling on the salesperson's behalf.

You see, deep down, people *love* to be helpful. Provided they are *asked* for help correctly. There are very few truly 'nasty bastards' around.

Transport cafés serve the same purpose as goods depots, except the prospects found tend to be national instead of local. Astute salespeople will lunch at transport cafés, get into conversation with a couple of lorry drivers and use exactly the same technique. Across the whole salesforce, leads gained from such sources would be fed into a central co-ordinator for redistribution to the territory concerned.

Minders!

A guy I met on holiday in the West Indies has a lovely idea for getting acquainted with new prospects. He sells time-sharing for a beachfront estate in Antigua. Some days, he quits the estate office and takes himself along the beach or on one of the tourist 'pirate cruises', dressed only in bathing trunks and flip-flops. Being a smoker, he carries a packet of cigarettes and a lighter in his hand.

He has an eye for likely prospects – couples who look like they've lived long enough to be able to afford what he's selling. When he finds a couple, he smiles down on them and says:

> 'Hey, I wonder, would you do me a great favour? I want to swim. Would you look after my cigarettes and lighter while I'm in the water?'

After the swim, getting into more meaningful conversation and inviting the couple to come and see his time-sharing units is a piece of cake.

If he's on board a cruise boat, the patter goes:

> 'Hey, I wonder, would you do me a great favour? I'm going to swim ashore, rather than take the dinghy. Would you take my cigarettes and lighter ashore with you?'

The Star Prize

The most glorious example of being different, the one to which I give my star prize, I came upon in 1978. It's never been surpassed.

The company in question had found that, within its list of good prospective customers, there were several hundred that were refusing even to grant its salespeople the opportunity to get face-to-face. 'Not interested', was the message even though research had proved that the company could improve those prospective customers' businesses no end.

The powers-that-be decided that something must be done about it. All that business going to waste just because the salesforce couldn't get in and start selling. But no one could crack the problem.

Then the publicity manager came up with what everyone considered was a really wild, mad idea. If there hadn't been so much business at stake, if the research hadn't been as thorough, it's doubtful that the idea would ever have got off the ground.

But it did.

The best 100 'not interested' prospective customers were selected. An order was placed with a top manufacturing jeweller for 100 specially designed gold medals, in velvet-lined presentation boxes. A calligrapher was commissioned to design and produce 100 parchment certificates, which were then framed – non-reflective glass and all. Total cost around £4,000 (1978 remember!).

With a suitable prestigious covering letter from the company's chairman, a gold medal and framed certificate were sent by courier to each of the 100 top prospects. The certificate contained these words:

ACME DISTRIBUTORS
MOST HARD TO GET AT
MAN OF THE YEAR
AWARD 1978

Presented to _____

for successfully avoiding the Acme Distributors salesforce

_____ Chairman

_____ Managing Director

This is really high psychology. The framed certificates by themselves would have got up most people's noses. It was the solid gold medals that did the trick. No one would go to that much trouble and expense if they were not sincere. There weren't many of the 100 certificates that weren't hung in prospective customers' offices immediately. Such people would consider the award a very high honour indeed. After all, they were all founder members of the 'We hate salespeople ' club. The gold medals had pride of place on their office desks.

Now for the results of the exercise. The salesforce didn't stop trying to get in, of course. In fact, they renewed their efforts with increased vigour. And this time they succeeded. Within three months of the presentation, 77 out of the 100 had been cracked.

Think about it. To who else but the representative of the company that had presented the award could those 100 prospects properly show their appreciation, and demonstrate that the award was being displayed in their office for all to see?

A very fruitful investment, the powers-that-be decided on review – but no one has done it since. Maybe the fluctuating price of gold has put this kind of 'being different' beyond reach.

So be different. Go on. You can do it if you put your mind to it. And it will demoralize your competitors dreadfully when they get to know about what you're doing.

Remember – when you are up against strong competition, you not only have to find more new customers, you have to find them before your competitors find them So it helps if you can slow your competitors down.

Chapter 2

How to Make 'Cold Canvassing' Productive

The managing director of the pump manufacturing company stands up and addresses his salesforce.

'All you've got to do', he tells them, 'is get out there and look for chimneys. Wherever there's a chimney, there's going to be a pump underneath it.'

The novice salesperson, one month into a new job, has been let out to call on a few customers 'to get the feet wet' after a couple of weeks in the sales office and the works, learning about the products. The salesperson encounters this huge sign at the entrance to a large industrial estate.

'Wow,' the salesperson thinks, 'a whole day's work with only 10 miles on the expense account. That'll please my manager.' And parks the company car, loads the briefcase with literature and proceeds to knock on doors.

The sales director has been examining his salesforce's call reports and expenses claims. His boardroom colleague in accounts bent his ear yesterday about the spiralling costs of telephone calls. Face-to-face selling time is 70 per cent of what it was this time last year. The salesforce spends on average one and a half days every week at home, making appointments, preparing proposals and planning ahead. He decides that a change of policy is required. He pens a memo to his salesforce:

> 'Far too much selling time is being spent at home, instead of with customers and prospective customers. Starting Monday, I want to see the number of sales calls made increasing by 20 per cent minimum. YCSSOYA!'

The customer's purchasing committee is holding its monthly meeting. All the executives with divisional and departmental buying responsibilities are present. The subject under discussion is time. The time the members of the purchasing committee spend talking to representatives of suppliers and potential suppliers.

> 'I had 17 salespeople asking to see me last week,' says one executive. 'None of them had an appointment and, out of the five I actually saw, only one knew anything about our business and what I was responsible for buying.'
>
> 'I can beat that,' says another executive. 'My secretary's been keeping a record since our last meeting. In the last month, we've had 94 representatives try to get to us without a prior appointment, 26 attempts to secure an appointment by suppliers we don't do business with, 18 attempts to sell over the telephone and 12 visits from people we do business with.'

Each of the members of the purchasing committee has similar figures. Each agrees that, in order to be effective as an executive with buying responsibilities, some suppliers' representatives must be seen. One must keep up-to-date with what's available and make regular checks on prices, quality, delivery, etc.

But the time available for talking to suppliers' representatives is strictly limited, and must be even more strictly limited in future. Everyone agrees.

Thus, the purchasing committee decides that a notice shall be displayed in the main reception area ...

... and the reception area staff are briefed on how to handle people from the pump manufacturer, novice salespeople and those discouraged by their companies from using their telephones to make appointments.

More and more 'By Appointment Only' notices are appearing in reception areas. More and more customers are demanding that salespeople make appointments and are refusing point-blank to see random callers – on principle. Time is money. Wasting that time talking to inept, unprepared salespeople is no longer acceptable to anyone other than inept, unprepared customers. If you want to plan your future growth around people like that, go ahead, but I bet you don't make the end of this book, or your sales and profit targets.

Cold Canvassing – the practice of knocking on prospective customers' doors, out of the blue, no appointment, no prior research – isn't a viable proposition any more for most businesses. This is something of a pity, because every good salesperson sometimes underruns on a planned call and finds himself 50 miles from the nearest known customer, and with an hour to spare.

The logical thing to do with that spare hour is to talk to a few receptionists about what their companies do, what they buy and who's responsible for the buying or the specifying. This amounts to research; detective work as discussed in the previous chapter, to pave the way for an effective, by appointment, call the *next* time you are in that section of your territory.

But wouldn't it be satisfying if, with the appropriate degree of professionalism and original thinking, the Cold Canvass call *could* be made viable again. Think how a few extra orders secured this way could bring you over target with no additional selling costs.

Here are a few ideas to get you thinking about how you could crack this problem. There is but one proviso – the prospective customers that you Cold Canvass must be businesses that should be able to use your products or services. This much research has to be done in all cases.

(To put you out of your misery, YCSSOYA stands for 'You can't sell sitting on your ...')

Business Cards with a Difference

Let's assume there are no 'By Appointment Only' notices to hold up progress. The average novice salesperson walks into the reception hall for a Cold Canvass call, presents a business card to the receptionist and asks to see the person who is responsible for buying or specifying, let's say widgets.

The receptionist takes the business card, rings through to the person responsible and says something like this:

'There's a Mr John Fenton here to see you.'

The reaction of the person responsible will, more often than not, be, 'What's he want?'

The receptionist, more often than not, will then take the line of least resistance. She has the salesperson's business card in her hand, so:

'It says here "Universal Widget Corporation – area representative,"'
she reads to the person responsible.

What an incredibly powerful carrot with which to hit the person responsible between the eyes. Awe-inspiring. He's so impressed, all he can think of saying is, 'Tell him I'm too busy. Get him to leave some literature'.

The receptionist looks up at the salesperson and says, 'He's too busy at the moment but if you'd like to leave some literature he'll be happy to look through it when he's got time'.

There's nowhere else to go. Leave the literature and say goodbye. Another abortive call. Yes it is; he'll never get round to reading the literature, even if it ever gets as far as his office.

Okay – if you reckon I'm being a touch over-dramatic, dig out your own business card, put yourself in the shoes of that person responsible and read it to yourself as if the receptionist were reading it. Bet you don't get face-to-face with yourself!

So the first rule for Cold Canvass calls is – don't use your business card unless it says something that will clearly come over as a dangled carrot. Just be yourself.

> 'My name's John Fenton, from Universal Widget Corporation. I'm after the person responsible for buying or specifying widgets in your company. Could you tell me who that is?'

She tells you.

> 'Will you find out from him if he can spare me 10 minutes, please?'

She contacts the person responsible. He still asks, 'What's he want?' But now she can't take the line of least resistance. She has to turn to you and say: 'He wants to know what you want'. So you say,

> 'Well, it's a bit complicated. Can I borrow your 'phone and explain to him myself? It'll be much easier.'

Now you're at exactly the same point where you would have been had you telephoned in advance for an appointment. So dangle the carrot and close.

> 'It'll only take you 10 minutes for us to establish whether we can give you a better deal or not. Can I see you now, or would you prefer me to call back later this morning, say, in an hour from now? I've got to see one of our customers just down the road, anyway.'

If you are very, very good, then on that one in a thousand Cold Canvass call you might find a straight personal challenge will get you face-to-face and further.

Stuart sells racking and shelving. One Friday afternoon approaching 5pm (there's a novelty!) he made a Cold Canvass call on a division of Walls Ice Cream. He didn't use his business card and swiftly found himself holding the receptionist's telephone and speaking to the works manager. After a few minutes of carrot dangling, the works manager said to Stuart, 'We're quite happy with our present suppliers and have been for the past 10 years.'

Stuart, quick on his feet, straight away replied, 'I've been eating Lyons Maid ice-cream with complete satisfaction for the past 26 years, but I'm willing to change if someone convinces me there's a better ice-cream.'

The works manager couldn't help laughing. 'All right, you so and so,' he said. 'Come up and talk to me.'

Stuart has since supplied several thousand pounds worth of racking and shelving to Walls, at no great difference in price or quality compared with the supplier the works manager said he's been happy with for the past 10 years.

Now wouldn't it be better if your business card dangled the carrot for you? Consider the fun you could get – and the business you could get – from your Cold Canvass calls if you used a card like this.

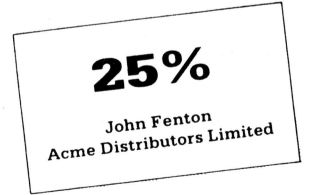

You walk into reception, ask for the name of the person responsible, hand the receptionist your card and say,

'Could Mr Green spare me 10 minutes?'

She rings through to Mr Green, gives your name and company and he says, 'What's he want?' She takes the line of least resistance and reads the card. 'It just says 25 per cent!'

Mr Green, maybe a touch irritably, asks 'What's that mean?' The receptionist turns to you and says, 'He wants to know what the 25 per cent means'. You simply reply,

'Well, that's the average amount we save our customers on warehousing costs if they use our products.'

'Oh,' she says, and goes back to Mr Green. 'He says it's what they usually save people who use their products – on warehousing costs.'

Now consider Mr Green's position. If he says to his company's receptionist, 'Tell him I'm too busy' he's declaring to a lesser employee that he doesn't care much about saving his company 25 per cent off anything. Is he likely to put himself in that position? No, he's not.

The worst that can happen to you is that you get face-to-face with Mr Green and he tells you to close the door quietly on the way out – in private!

The 25 per cent business card has another, equally powerful use. Note it does not have a telephone number.

Say you have compiled a list of suspects or prospects and you are approaching the stage of first contact. Icy cold will be the usual reception when you telephone for an appointment – you can't use the 25 per cent gambit on the telephone. But you still know that an appointment is more professional than just dropping in, even with ammunition like the 25 per cent card.

So you address small envelopes to each name on your suspect/prospect list, write on the back of your 25 per cent cards,

'Please ring me on 01789 266716' and post just a 25 per cent card to each person, in the envelope, on its own, by itself!

Curiosity does the rest. You're likely to get a 99 per cent response. And when they ring *you*, they're warm, not icy cold. They ask the question direct – 'What does this 25 per cent mean?' and off you go.

Think of the economics as well as the fun – you've spent money on a stamp and an envelope, but your *prospect* is paying for the telephone call.

If you're selling to retailers and department stores, consider this second example which you could hand to a counter assistant to take to the manager or department buyer:

The four top-priority objectives for any retailer: profit, throughput, quality and price competitiveness. How could any store manager given this card by one of his assistants send back a message via that assistant, 'Tell him I'm too busy,' without risking the word going round that he didn't care any more?

Titles

Still on the subject of business cards, a very effective force for getting in on a Cold Canvass call is to carry the highest possible title. If you are a managing director, this title on your card will get you face-to-face with just about anyone, with or without an appointment. But how many managing directors make Cold Canvass calls?

One London-based wholesaler, fed up with the number of times its five salespeople were turned away by its retailer prospective customers, decided to trade in the salespeople's Minis and replace them with Jaguars and gave them business cards carrying the title 'Sales Director'.

As a direct result, sales increased ten-fold in two years.

Put Yourself in the Customer's Shoes

That's a very important thing to be able to do if you want to be a successful salesperson in a competitive market place. But in the context of successful Cold Canvassing, I use it to mean that you should assume the role of a customer when you walk into that prospective customer's reception hall. When prospective customers walk into suppliers' premises out of the blue, they get a totally different reception from that given to salespeople who walk in out of the blue, don't they?

Don't they?…

Here is an example of a 'Customer's Shoes' cold canvassing technique for a machine tool company. The company sold very expensive computerized turning machines with very high production rates and component quality.

The first objective for the company's sales engineers was to find out what kind of components a prospective customer was producing, in what quantity, at what level of quality and on what kind of machines. The most effective way to establish all this essential information was to get into the prospective customer's machine shop and see it happening. But getting the prospective customer's works manager to let them into the factory was something the sales engineers found somewhat difficult.

52

So we drew up an A4-size card on which was printed sectional drawings of a representative selection of the kind of components that the company's turning machines were best at producing.

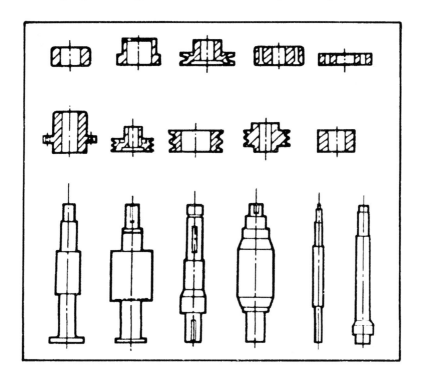

The sales engineer walks into the prospective customer's reception hall. He has the components card in his hand and his survey pad. No briefcase. A briefcase at this stage would be a dead giveaway. He bids the receptionist good morning.

'Could you ask your works manager if he could spare me 10 minutes. My name is John Fenton. I want to find out if you make anything like these.'

The receptionist looks at the card and doesn't know if its owner is selling or buying. If she asks, 'Are you buying or selling?' the sales engineer replies, 'I hope to be instrumental in increasing your business quite substantially'.

She rings through to the works manager. He comes out to reception and the sales engineer shows him the components card. 'Do you make anything that looks remotely like any of these?'

The works manager is immediately locked in on the card. He can't help himself.

'Er, well, we do something like that, and like that, and a few now and again like that,' he says, pointing to the appropriate sectional drawings on the card.

'What material do you make them in? Do you have to put them through a grinding operation to get the necessary surface finish? What sizes of batches? What kind of machines do you produce them on? Do you use numerical control or computerized numerical control, at all?'

The picture that the sales engineer builds from the answers to these questions very quickly takes shape. 'Wow,' he says, 'I might be wrong, but I reckon we could cut your machine shop production and labour costs as far as turning and grinding is concerned by probably 50 per cent, and double your capacity if you're looking for more work. Could I take another 10 minutes of your time and get you to let me have a look at your machine shop?'

More often than not, the works manager's curiosity and appetite are aroused. 'Don't see why not – follow me,' he says and off they go.

As a guest speaker at a sales conference held by TNT Overnite – the express parcels delivery service, for a bit of fun, I built a fairly large parcel, wrapped round with metres of TNT Overnite adhesive tape. Inside the parcel was a small cassette tape recorder, and I'd put into the cassette a recording of a very loud, very tinny, ticking alarm clock.

Amplified by the tape recorder, the ticking sounded pretty urgent!

Thus, I made my entrance and did my thing. The ticking parcel achieved a resounding ovation, and my opening words, 'If you walked into a prospective customer's premises, out of the blue, carrying one of these, and asked to speak to the Despatch Manager, what would be the reaction of the receptionist?' were developed into 10 minutes of highly productive discussion.

'Forget the ticking clock,' the conference decided. 'What would be the reaction if you just walked in with an urgent parcel?' You wouldn't look like a sales person any more, you'd look like a customer. Almost certainly, you'd get face-to-face with the Despatch Manager – cold canvass – in minimum elapsed time.'

I left that conference deliberating on how to disguise all the salesforce's briefcases as TNT Overnite parcels!

The Jekyll-and-Hyde Technique

There are some areas of Selling where teamwork pays better dividends than the lone approach, especially in Cold Canvassing. Two salespeople, working in partnership, can break down barriers that the single salesperson often finds insurmountable

Take Double Glazing and Replacement Windows, sold direct to householders by salespeople on commission only. Arthur and George decide to team up. On one particular day, they Cold Canvass a particular housing estate. They tackle a street at a time, Arthur knocking on doors on one side, George the other side.

'Good morning', says Arthur to the lady of the house. 'I'm from UWC Double Glazing. We're conducting a market survey of houses on this estate, to find out how many of them are already fitted with double glazing or secondary glazing. Can I ask you a few questions about your house?'

A few questions further on and Arthur figures this particular house is a good prospect. But he also knows that, having started in with the Market Survey technique, he cannot now switch over and start selling. To do so would send the prospective customer shrieking into the night. This is where the teamwork comes in.

'If I might make a suggestion,' says Arthur. 'We've produced a video film of what we've been doing in this and other areas to make houses like yours a lot more comfortable to live in at very little expense, especially in noisy districts. I know my colleague George Ratcliffe is in this district next Tuesday evening. If Tuesday is a convenient evening for both you and your husband, I could get in touch with Mr Ratcliffe and have him bring over the video film to show you. It only takes about 20 minutes. He's got a video player, if you haven't got one yourself. You'll probably enjoy seeing how easy it is to play video through your telly as much as seeing our film. What would be the best time on Tuesday evening – around 7.30 or would you prefer a bit later?'

George Ratcliffe is busy on the other side of the street, checking out houses and making appointments for Arthur for next Tuesday evening. On Tuesday, they're both back, but on opposite sides of the street.

This Jekyll-and-Hyde technique can be applied to any reasonably compact area and used for office equipment, computers, vending machines, carpet cleaning, cars, in fact any product or service where a market survey can be credibly conducted.

Cold Canvassing by Telephone

So far, we've looked at the kind of productive Cold Canvassing that comes from face-to-face calls. Many businesses, however, find that the Cold Canvass element is best tackled by well-trained office-based people, whose job is to conduct a telephone market survey and, if the suspect turns into a prospect by the end of the survey, to fix appointments on behalf of the field salesforce.

This kind of Cold Canvassing is a systematic, full-time job, where the suspect lists are derived from directories or computer bureaux databases. The telephone surveyors sit at specially constructed desks with acoustic panels all around them, and the panels bear checklists of the best things to say to prospects who show resistance, without upsetting the prospect and to achieve the objective in spite of the resistance.

Such telephone survey teams run daily, weekly and monthly competitions for those who book the most appointments, with penalty points for any that subsequently prove useless by the time the field salesperson has visited the prospect. In this way, morale within the tele-team and co-operation between the tele-team and the field salesforce are maintained at a very high level, as are results.

If you're wondering why you're in a business that doesn't have any directories or computer databases that can be used for activities like this, I can put your mind at rest. There are directories, guides, yearbooks, trade association membership lists, professional body membership lists, specialist bureaux and computer print-outs for every kind of business, as well as countless sources of information on the internet. You just haven't found one for yours yet.

Keep looking. There are over 2000 different directories published each year in the UK alone. Two of them are directories of *directories*, published by CBD Research Ltd of Beckenham, Kent, and British Rate and Data, MacLean Hunter Ltd, London. Two more are directories of available mailing lists, published by Gower Press Ltd (*The Direct Mail Databook*) and Benn Brothers (*Benn's Direct Marketing Services Directory*).

To whet your appetite with a few specific examples – if you are looking for scrap merchants there is the *European Scrap Directory*. If you are after property developers, there is the *Property Directory*. If you sell welding rods for strange materials, maybe the *Stainless Steel Fabricators Directory* will do you some good. If you cater for coalmines, *The Guide to the Coal Fields* gives you everything in the UK, even maps. If you want to sell rubber truncheons, *The Police and Constabulary Almanac* is a must.

Once in a Lifetime – Yorick from Warwick!

Once in a lifetime, you get the opportunity to develop something that really is unbeatable. It happened to me, and it happened by chance.

My wife bought me a somewhat unusual birthday present – a human skull, about 150 years old, mounted on a plinth, with the cranium neatly cut all round and hinged, so that the brain cavity could be inspected. Obviously it had been in the hands of a medical student at some time in the past.

Being born of Stratford-upon-Avon and still resident in the Bard's borough, my skull was christened **Yorick**. Yorick became potentially the most powerful Selling Tool ever invented, capable, in the right hands, of increasing both face-to-face selling time and orders by 1000 per cent on Cold Canvass calls.

Yorick has appeared many times on television and has been put through his paces (the skull *is* a 'he'!) in front of more than 250,000 salespeople. I have personally tested his effectiveness in six different real-life situations and he has a 100 per cent success record – so far.

Yorick performs best when he's selling the latest kind of pocket calculator; one that, when you push the buttons, actually speaks what you have pushed: 'Nine zero four divided by two zero equals four five point two'. The calculator, in its PVC case, fits snugly into Yorick's brain cavity.

So picture the real-life selling situation. A crowded retail shop, the kind that sells calculators, cameras, stationery and what have you. A dozen or so customers. The manager and his assistant all busy serving. The kind of situation where, if you were selling into that type of retail shop, you have to wait patiently until the customers have been served before you stand a hope of getting five minutes of the manager's time – and where, as customers go out, more keep coming in. You could be stuck there waiting for an hour.

But now you have Yorick to help you. He's under your right arm as you walk into the shop. Your briefcase is in your left hand. You stop in the centre of the shop. You just stand there, saying nothing. All conversation stops in three seconds flat. Deathly silence. All eyes are focused on Yorick. The manager of the shop is the first to speak.

He says, 'Excuse me for a moment' to the customer he is serving, walks up to you and commits the cardinal sin of retail or exhibition selling. He says 'Can I help you, sir?'

You put your briefcase down, pat Yorick on the top of his head and say, loud enough for everyone in the shop to hear, 'In here, is the nearest thing to the human brain that's so far been developed. Let me show you.'

You walk to the nearest counter, set Yorick down and open his cranium. If you're unlucky, the oldest customer will faint. You take out your Speaking Pocket Calculator, making sure the volume control is turned up to maximum, and proceed to demonstrate. 'Eight five two divided by three multiplied by one six equals four five four four.'

'That's fantastic, how much is it?' one of the customers in the shop is certain to say, because of course you've demonstrated your calculator to everyone in the shop. Another strong possibility is 'Ooo, just what I need for my nephew's birthday!'

'It retails at £59.50, including the leather case, batteries and full instructions,' you explain to the customer. Then you turn to the manager and say casually, 'I've got three in my briefcase and some more in my car down the road. How many would you like for stock?'

That's *really* productive Cold Canvassing.

My big problem now is that I've got to find something even better than Yorick. The unbeatable must be beaten. That's the kind of challenge I like.

Psst. It's all changed!

No good just sitting there.

Okay, so you hate change.

Just remember, it's the only thing in life (other

than death) that's permanent.

Sit there much longer,

and your competitors will

have it all. They've been

changing for quite some time now.

Get off your bottom!

JF

Chapter 3

How to Stop Competitors Stealing Your Customers

Consider this notice, seen more in restaurants than anywhere else.

Such notices are tributes to a belief in the power of word-of-mouth communication and referral. But few people realize just how powerful word-of-mouth communication really is – or realize how much it can damage, or build, a business.

Coca-Cola commissioned some research in the US to try to measure this power. The firm that conducted the research, Technical

Assistance Research Programs Inc. of Washington, talked to 1,717 Coca-Cola customers (the stores, not the drinkers!) and found that:

- customers who had complained and who felt their complaints had not been satisfactorily resolved, talked about their complaint to between nine and ten other people;
- customers who had complained and who were *completely satisfied* with the response to their complaint, talked about their complaint to between four and five other people.

Think about these statistics. Think about how susceptible these customers are to the overtures and advances of your competitors. That your business is different from Coca-Cola's doesn't matter much. Don't kid yourself this doesn't apply to you. Surely it would be less expensive to prevent migration by resolving the complaints of existing customers than to win new customers? But how about doing *both*? That's *really* winning! Especially against competition.

The Coca-Cola research also covered inquiries as well as complaints, and discovered that:

- customers who had made inquiries and felt they had *not* received satisfactory answers, talked about it to between four and five other people;
- customers who had made inquiries and were satisfied with the answers, talked about it to between three and four other people.

Proof again that bad news travels fastest and furthest.

Consider how much *more* difficult it would be to sell to newly found prospects if they happened to be one of those nine and ten, or four and five other people. Don't neglect this critical and very grey area of your business.

**YOU NEVER GET A SECOND CHANCE
TO MAKE A FIRST IMPRESSION.**

Robert Townsend, while chief executive of Avis-Rent-A-Car, set up the best way I know of tackling the complaints problem. He passed it on to all in his fantastically successful books *Up the Organization* and *Further Up the Organisation* (Michael Joseph).

With his and his publisher's permission (but you should still buy his books) I pass his words on to you.

Chairman of the Executive Committee

Most companies are doing it all wrong. They're wasting this title and others like it on retired brass. These titles can be very useful.

A certain National Institute was created recently. It has a young director with a good deal of experience in the field, but not much experience in managing an organization. He had his objectives clearly thought out and budgets prepared showing how and where he hoped to reach them and what it would mean to the industry. But it was already clear that one of his problems was going to be visits and phone calls from international visiting firemen and from people in the industry wanting to talk to the boss.

He had no room in his budget for an assistant and, besides, people won't be pushed off on an assistant. He did have a substantial expense account for entertainment. So he called up an old friend who was retired and said, "I can't pay you a salary, but if you'll come and take all these phone calls and lunches and dinners off my back, I'll make you Chairman of the Executive Committee. You can have some fun and meet some interesting people and I can spend all my time getting the Institute going."

The key is in the title. Nobody knows what it means. It can mean much or nothing. But nobody ever gets mad when the boss says, "Let me switch you to the Chairman of our Executive Committee – this is the kind of thing he takes charge of".

I've seen this work in an area like customer complaints. People who write or call with complaints want someone to listen, sympathize, apologise and, if indicated, correct the matter. And the higher up their complaint is handled the quicker their fire goes out.

But companies still insist on having these complaints handled by "customer services departments" or "complaints departments". If I'm switched to one of these, I'm twice as mad as when I called. But I'm docile as a lamb if I hear, "Let me transfer you to the Chairman of the

Executive Committee. One of his people will take care of you. He likes to hear about all the complaints."

I could be talking to the same clerk in the same department (except now he is speaking for the Chairman of the Executive Committee). And the letter of apology on that glorious letterhead not only rubs out my grievance, it retains me as a customer and gives me something to brag about to your other prospects.

Complaints Handling

There is a tried and tested method for dealing properly with company complaints whether or not you are blessed with a 'Chairman of the Executive Committee'. It goes like this:

1. When customers complain about something, don't ever side with them against your company. (However you do this, whether you switch from 'we' to 'they' or from 'us' to 'them', you'll be suggesting to these customers that this sort of thing is always happening and that if they were a bit brighter, they would deal elsewhere).

2. Never, never, never take the complaints personally. It's not you they're having a go at, it's the product, the service or the company. Stay cool.

3. Thank the customers for bringing the problems to your notice and for giving you the opportunity to put things right. (But don't ever patronize.)

4. Tell the customers you are sorry they have been upset. (But don't apologise on behalf of your company at this stage for having done something wrong. You don't even know whose fault it is, yet!)

5. Get the full story down on paper. (If the customers gets everything

off their chests in one go, you'll have a much easier time.)

6. Never interrupt, or argue, or justify. (But you can ask a few questions to clarify any areas of doubt.)

7. Tell the customers what action you are going to take. Get them to agree to it. *Then take it.* (And keep them informed.)

The Ostrich Complex

A lot of complaints mountains grow out of mole hills right across Selling because of the Ostrich Complex – the practice of burying one's head in the sand until the problem has gone away. But, of course, the problem never does go away. A lot of these kinds of complaints are caused by late deliveries. (If your company suffers regularly from this problem, get hold of a book by Sydney Paulden entitled *How to Deliver on Time* (Gower Press).

If deliveries are going to be late, salespeople have a plain, simple duty to the customers to tell them *fast.* Give the customers as much notice as possible, so that they can change their own schedules or arrangements.

You will still get a rocket which will turn both your ears red, but that is far, far better than to say absolutely nothing and then have your customer telephone a few days *after* the scheduled delivery date to enquire, 'Where the hell is it ...?' and have to say, 'Oh, er ... I'm sorry, but, er ... it's going to be another six weeks'.

A salesperson who does that doesn't deserve customers, and certainly isn't going to win *this* business battle.

The Odds

Never underestimate the Competition. Most salespeople are up against very poor odds. No bookmaker would take money on their chances of success – whether it's retaining existing customers or winning new customers.

If ten suppliers are sharing a particular market, then for every salesperson trying to keep and protect a particular customer, there are nine other salespeople trying to steal that customer away. Most prospects are someone else's customer. So every salesperson to whom this is being done is, at the same time, doing this to someone else.

Motivation guru Douglas McGregor conducted some experiments. He took a number of 'representative samples' of people, several bunches of students of similar mix, and communicated to them some ideas which they accepted. Then, after a couple of days, he subjected the same representative sample bunches to another person, who communicated to them some entirely different ideas on the same subject.

He found that 80 per cent of the people in the representative samples changed their minds and opted for the second set of ideas.

McGregor then took a similar number of completely new 'representative samples', although the people were the same kind of people. He conducted the entire exercise again, but this time, at the end of his first communication, he added something. He told each bunch that in a couple of days, another person would come to see them, would give them some entirely different ideas and would try to make them change their minds.

The other person duly did his thing, but this time, only 20 per cent changed their minds.

The ramifications of McGregor's tests are mind-bending! It is obviously possible to build mental barriers in people's minds which reject advances from competitors. A natural resistance to change – something that your existing customers should all have to a very advanced degree, but that your prospective customers and you yourself should *never* suffer from.

How do you build such mental barriers and resistance in a Selling situation? Well, you don't knock the competition, that's for sure. Do that and you're back in the crowd.

You sell the Difference – the USP (see *Selling – the Most Important Job in the World*, John Fenton; Management Books 2000) – and you reinforce the difference at every opportunity, reminding your customers of all the benefits they're getting by buying from you.

'You can get this product cheaper, of course, but then you wouldn't be getting the extra reliability and longer life, or our design service.'

'Bloggs make very good pumps, but you're getting some very important extras from us that you wouldn't get from Bloggs. Our multiflexible coupling, for example. How would your chaps cope without that? And our automatic declogger.'

You can even quote generalities like:

'There's nothing in the world that can't be made just a little cheaper – and just a little worse.'

Or ask questions like:

'If you were an astronaut, about to blast off for the Moon, and you learnt that the million components making up your space capsule had all been bought on the basis of the lowest price, how would you feel?'

Rumours

Way back in the days before laptops and PCs, there were only about five major main-frame computer manufacturers competing for the very big business, the highly specialized business, at the top end of the market.

The market itself, in Britain, totalled only about 30 key decision-makers. A rumour was spread, no one knows whether deliberately or not, to the effect that one of the big five computer manufacturers was planning to pull out of the UK market, due to a fall-off in demand and insufficient profits.

Within days, all 30 of the key decision-makers had got wind of the rumour. As a result, that manufacturer didn't get one enquiry from the market for almost a year. No one was prepared to take the risk.

A true story about a totally untrue rumour.

Do your competitors spread rumours about you and your company? If they do, what action do you take?

Here's another true story, which shows you what action you *could* take.

A company in the materials handling industry was based at Grays, in Essex, the flat bit of the Thames estuary. One summer evening, half the county of Essex was subjected to a sudden and incredibly savage cloudburst. Three hours of the heaviest rain anyone had ever seen. The drains and sewers couldn't take it. Manholes blew everywhere. Roads were washed away. Landslides and widespread flooding.

A day later, only the debris was left. The water had gone.

A month later, a rumour began to spread about the materials handling company at Grays. Competitors' salespeople were saying to customers and prospective customers: 'Hey, you want to be careful if you do business with ... their factory gets flooded out pretty regularly and you know what water does to this kind of equipment'.

The management of the Grays company happened to be fast on its feet. A light aircraft was hired for a day and a photographer sent up to take pictures of the factory and the surrounding area. The most suitable picture was selected and prints run off for each of the salespeople.

A meeting was held to brief the salespeople on how to use the pictures. They were told to talk about the rumour, the flood and show the picture, on every single call they made, *at the beginning of the call*. A fly on the wall probably heard this:

'You know, Mr Jones, it's incredible the lengths our competitors go to, to try to discredit us. There's a rumour they're spreading now that our factory floods every month. Actually, it got flooded out in that cloudburst a few weeks back, along with just about every other factory in Essex, but look at this.' *(Salesperson brings out aerial photo of factory)*

'Here's our factory. Here's the river Thames, half a mile away. And, look, running all the way from Dagenham to Southend, unbroken, is this railway embankment. Now I ask you, how the hell could our factory get flooded?'

End of story; beginning of business discussion.

If you're still a fly on the wall of Mr Jones' office a few days later, when one of the competitors tries spreading the rumour, you'd see Mr Jones lean back in his chair, fold his arms and wait for the salesperson to finish his knocking. Then you'd hear Mr Jones ask:

'Have you ever seen that factory down at Grays?'
'Er, no. Why do you ask?'
'Because it's half a mile from the river Thames and there's a bloody great railway embankment running continuously between the two. So how do you reckon their factory gets flooded?'

The salesperson goes bright red from neck to forehead, and the rest of the visit is a disaster.

After two months of the Grays' salesforce using the aerial photograph on every call they made, not only did the rumour disappear, the company was stronger, compared with its competitors, than it had ever been.

Hoisted with own petard, I call that. And a lot of fun while you're doing it.

Taking Advantage

Be careful not to give your competitors an opportunity to steal your existing customers.

Here's an example from the printing industry. One of the major suppliers of lithographic printing plates found it had a strike on its hands and saw fit to inform *its* customers. A letter duly went out.

Dear Sirs,

As you may be aware, employees engaged in the manufacture of lithographic printing plates and chemicals are in membership of the National Graphical Association.

Regrettably, I have to advise you that the NGA have given us notice of their intention to support a withdrawal of labour with effect from Monday, 29 June.

This stoppage is particularly disturbing since the company's offer had previously been recommended for acceptance by the National Executive Council of the NGA who are now giving official backing to industrial action in pursuit of the wage claim.

Whilst we can appreciate an individual's aspirations, in these matters the cumulative effect of excessive wage settlements cannot be in the interests of the industry, or those whom it employs; one would have hoped that the events of the last year would have been evidence enough.

As a British company, and a major supplier to the UK printing industry, we believe that we have a responsibility to provide satisfying, rewarding jobs for those in our employ; we also believe that we have no less a responsibility to the industry to play our part in maintaining a reliable product, dependable service and stable prices, and it must be borne in mind that the offer in dispute is in line with the settlements recently concluded in the printing industry. So whilst we apologise for any temporary inconvenience or interruption of supply, we trust that you will bear with us and we hope we can resume normal service as quickly as possible. If in the meantime you require assistance or advice please contact your local depot.

Yours faithfully

Two days later, one of the company's major competitors sent out a letter to all the relevant printers, offering to provide plates during the strike.

Dear Sir,

Pre-sensitized aluminium offset litho plates

I understand that one of our competitors has circularized the printing industry concerning their inability to supply offset plates due to industrial action.

Whilst I have no particular enthusiasm for capitalizing on another's misfortune, I am very conscious of the fact that you will need a supply of plates if you are to keep your presses running, otherwise more print work will go overseas. I am also concerned that you continue to use plates manufactured in Britain as your alternative source.

As the largest supplier of positive working offset plates to the UK market may I reassure you that we will be able to satisfy your requirements whatever the size. Also there is little likelihood of us being unable to supply due to industrial action.

You may recall that we have recently installed a new production line, which is generally regarded as being the most sophisticated plate-manufacturing unit in the Western world. As well as improving the quality of our products this new line also gave us a significant increase in capacity.

We may also be able to supply negative plates in limited sizes and quantities but positive working plates are definitely our lead products.

The ... range of positive plates is fully described by the enclosed literature.

All these plates are compatible with most brands of positive developer although best results are obtained using ... Positive Developer.

So, if you are worried about the continuity of your plate supplies, just give us a call at Head Office or any of our Branches.

Yours faithfully

As a result, the competitor acquired a considerable slice of the strike-bound company's business – and kept quite a bit of it long after the strike had ended.

There are lessons to be learned here!

We've got strengths and

we've got weaknesses – but

so have our competitors.

If we sell our strengths

against their weaknesses,

we'll win.

Chapter 4

How to Win Business From Your Competitors

If you want to win more business from your competitors, then – in the eyes of their customers – you've got to come over better than your competitors; more professional than your competitors. And the difference has got to be significant, not marginal.

For example, consider the record files you keep, full of the paperwork appertaining to the customer with whom you are face-to-face. How do you come over to that customer if you were visibly armed with that kind of documentation about the relationship so far? Is the customer impressed? Is the customer more impressed than with the way your competitors do business?

There are many ways you can come over better. You can show a greater concern for the customer's time. You can get to the point faster, impress him with your efficiency. You can even get the customer to tell you how *you* can achieve your objective of winning business from the competitor who's getting the business at present.

Let us assume you have done some research and found that a particular company uses widgets, but you haven't been able to dig up a carrot or establish any more tangible objective than, 'I want to sell this company some widgets'. You make contact with the key decision-maker, preferably face-to-face, but by telephone will do, and you say:

'Good morning, Mr Jones. As I understand it, your company uses a lot of widgets. (pause) My company sells widgets. Very good ones. I'd very much like to see you using some of ours. Please may I ask you a very direct question?
'What do I need to do to get you to buy some of your widgets from us?'

73

The last line is what I call 'the most powerful question in Selling'. Learn to use it well, and your order book will always be full. But don't smile when you use it. You must come over to the customer with complete sincerity. You really want to know – it's the most important thing in your life.

In some cases, the final question in the sequence might be:

'What do we need to do to get on your list of approved suppliers?'

Whatever the customer suggests you do, you can add a bit of confirmation and commitment before you actually do it:

'Fair enough. If we can do that, will you place some of your business our way?'

You'll find, as you become more and more proficient at competitive selling, that those three little words – 'if we can ...' – unlock more doors than you thought possible.

You can also attempt to quantify the business:

'How much of your business would you be able to move to us? How soon? What sizes?'

Now all you need to do is what the customer suggested you do. Do it to the customer's complete satisfaction, and the business must be yours.

Do you suffer from little tin god customers who keep you all to themselves but don't buy much from you – they place most of their business with a competitor?

The 'what do I have to do' technique is superb with that kind of person. There is another problem, however. Those little tin gods keep you away from other important contacts you should be making in that company. Remember – you're chasing business; you're not there just to keep little tin gods happy. The average number of people who exert influence on a decision to buy something, or change a supplier, increases as the size of the customer increases. In small companies, most decisions will be taken by one person, the boss. In very large companies the trend is more and more towards buying by committee.

If you want to win more business than your competitors, you've got to make sure you talk to more decision-makers and influencers than they do. If you don't, you'll come second again. A survey some years ago produced these figures on decision influencers. The survey covered 1100 British companies across a wide spread of industries.

Size of company (Number of employees)	Average number of decision influencers	Average number of influencers who talk to salespeople
Less than 200	3.43	1.72
201 to 400	4.85	1.75
401 to 1000	5.81	1.90
More than 1001	6.50	1.65
The trends	Steadily increasing	Static

If a little tin god gets in your way, you've got to find a way to gently, but firmly, move him to one side. Not easy, but here's one way to achieve this – and to continue the process of appearing better in the customer's eyes.

The Purchasing Cycle Plan

You ask a question:

'By the way, do you have a copy of your purchasing cycle plan handy? I wonder if I could have a copy?'

Every company goes about its requisitioning and purchasing of goods and services in a certain way. More often than not, there is a standard procedure laid down. This standard procedure, if translated into diagram form, is the 'purchasing cycle plan'. But rarely is the standard procedure translated into diagram form, so the usual reaction to your question will be:

'What do you mean, purchasing cycle plan?'

Great! Just the reaction you wanted. The opportunity to explain:

'Just a chart, a picture, in flow-diagram form, of how your company operates in respect of requisitioning and purchasing its supplies.

'I wanted it because we make a point of learning as much about how our customers operate as we can. That way, we can give the best possible service. Often, we can adjust our own standard procedures to dovetail exactly into a customer's standard procedures.'

Then you dive into your briefcase and pull out a couple of examples of purchasing cycle plans – one for *your own company's* purchasing department and the other for one of your better customers.

You explain how your own purchasing department operates, how it uses its disciplines and procedures to make sure customers are never let down on deliveries through hold-ups in the supply of components or materials. You explain how the cycle plan for your customer has helped you give that customer a better service and how it helped you pin-point an area where greater efficiency could be, and was, achieved.

And all the time, this customer you're talking to is thinking:

'This salesperson's a lot different from the usual rubbish that I have to see. His company seems to appreciate customers, too. Hmmm! Maybe I should try them out. This plan idea's not bad, either. I could use one of them. Do me some good with the boss.'

At an appropriate time in your explanation, you say:

'Does your cycle plan look anything like these? If you haven't got one in this form, can we draw it out now, on my pad?'

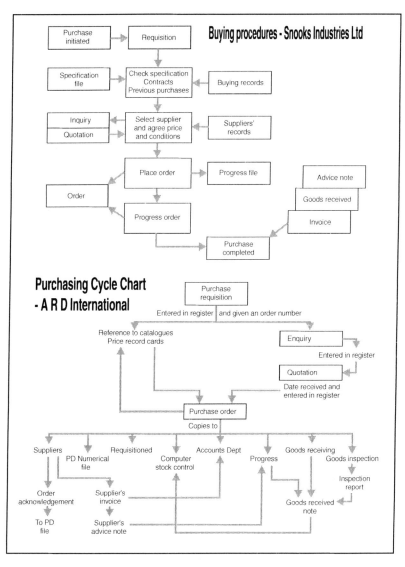

And before you know it, you and the customer are building his purchasing cycle plan on your A4 size survey pad. (A pocket notebook is useless!) Now you can start asking questions about each bit of the plan as it develops.

'What does this do?', 'How does this bit operate?', 'Who is involved in this section?', 'Who actually does the requisitioning?', 'Who actually signs the order?'

With some adroit questions during the drawing up of the purchasing cycle plan, most of those hitherto hidden decision influencers can be uncovered, and your little tin gods have very little opportunity to object to your talking to them from that point.

When the plan is completed, you thank the customer, and go to put it in your briefcase. What is guaranteed at this point is that the customer will say: 'Hang on, can I take a copy of that before you go away with it?'

That's competitive salespersonship!

But don't go mad and walk out with *just* the purchasing cycle plan instead of with an order. This is just the preliminary stage. Hang in there. You've still got work to do.

Short-circuiting the Politics

There is another way to go over the head of the little tin god without giving offence. That is to bring in your biggest gun – your managing director. (If you have a managing director who doesn't see himself as a big gun to help his salesforce, you've got big problems all round and I don't think I or anyone else can help you until he moves on. Hopefully, your company will still be in business when he does.)

The opening goes like this:

'My managing director would like to come in and talk to your production director. He's asked me to fix a meeting. I think he has a few things up his sleeve that could save you a fair bit of money. Can we fix up a convenient date and time, and include you in the meeting?'

You'll be there too. This top brass gambit will always overcome the political problems, and such a meeting should always end with the order being secured, or a firm commitment for the future.

But the truly incredible thing about this business isn't the number of managing directors who won't back up their salespeople when it's necessary – it's the vast majority of salespeople who won't call in the managing director when it's necessary. It's their ego, screwing up yet another piece of business they could have won.

Not long ago, I heard about a 'big gun' attack that won an order *after* a customer had placed the same order with a competitor *and* paid a deposit of £1,800 to the competitor.

The product was a piece of metal finishing machinery – a kind of rumbling barrel with knobs on.

Our hero, the salesperson who had found that he had lost the order to the competitor, reported this calamity to his sales director.

The sales director said, 'Hang on a minute; we've got one of these in stock. What delivery are the competition offering on this?'

'Six weeks minimum', replied the salesperson. 'So all is definitely not lost', said the sales director. 'Come on, let's go and talk to the customer.

Face-to-face with the customer's works manager a short while later, the sales director was proving on paper that a reduction of four weeks in the time before the machinery ordered could be in production represented savings to the customer amounting to a lot more than the £1,800 they'd paid as a deposit. 'Cancel the order and place it with us,' the sales director suggested.

'Can't really do that,' said the works manager, plainly worried. 'A deal is a deal. I doubt if our managing director would wear that.'

'Well, let's go and ask him,' said the sales director. 'There's a lot of money at stake, and you know you could do with this equipment ASAP.'

Upstairs to the managing director's office – all the way through the calculations again – and one final offer from the sales director – a discount on the ongoing consumables which went in the machinery, so that the customer could recoup his £1,800 deposit over his first 12 months purchases of the consumables. The deal was clinched – the first order cancelled. And the competitor was, of course, hopping mad. They tried everything, but the more they tried, the worse they made their position. In the end, their company was declared 'persona non grata' by the customer.

So when is an order really lost to the competition?

Being seen to be *better* than your competitors can come in all shapes and sizes. Here are some examples.

Be Better By Being Different

Let's go back to 1936, to a survey of 1000 salespeople's reports over a one-year period. (Yes, they did have to submit reports in 1936.) The survey totted up the number of times common excuses for not selling appeared in those 1000 reports.

Due to slump (now they call it recession)	86
Workers on short time	50
Christmas holidays	140
Summer holidays	70
Easter holidays	35
Tax bill to pay	176
No budget until next financial year	134
No money	93
Weather conditions!!	66
That's a total, out of 1000, of	850

I bet if you analyse your excuses for not selling over the past year, you won't find much difference. You're not even being original! The same excuses have been used since selling began.

Your management, quite often, doesn't help you overcome the excuses barrier, because negative thinking prevails in management just as much as it does at the sharp end.

Sales managers are often heard saying things like this:

'The product can't be sold at certain times of the year.'
'The product can't be sold in certain districts.'
'Trade is only seasonal.'
'You can't make calls the day before Bank Holiday.'
'Buyers place few orders during the first week of the new year.'

'Our salespeople don't take orders.
'It's no good calling before 10am, or after 4.30pm or on Friday afternoons; they won't see you.
'Large companies will only see you by appointment.'
'You can't get orders on Saturday mornings.'

What utter rubbish. All of it. Yes you can. Who made the rules anyway? What rules? As Sir Barnes Wallis used to say, 'Why not, why not?'

To beat your competitors, do all the things the average salesperson won't do and, every day, do at least one thing you don't want to do.

Be different, and from the difference, come over better.

You can't get orders on Saturday mornings? Of course you can in retail and Direct Selling. In Industrial Selling it is more difficult, certainly, because the customers don't normally work on Saturdays any longer. But one saleswoman cracked the problem.

Her name is Flo Wright, and at the time of this story she was manager of a machine tool distributor's showroom in the centre of Bristol. Her showroom had its own large car park and was right next to the MFI warehouse and the main shopping centre. Parking a car in the centre of Bristol on a Saturday for shopping is murder.

So, Flo decided to open for business on Saturdays. She had printed a quantity of car park passes and sent them out with a covering letter to all her customers and prospective customers. The letter read:

'If you shop in Bristol on Saturdays, you know how difficult it is to park your car. We have a large car park right next to the main shopping centre, and we are making it available to selected regular customers on Saturdays. Enclosed is your car park pass. If you show this to the car park attendant he will let you in.'

Quite a number of Flo's customers and prospective customers took her up on the offer. Good relations very well cemented. But Flo didn't stop there. She knew how husbands quickly develop 'shopping legs' and fall over with fatigue on Saturdays when out with their wives.

Ergonomically, the shortest route from her car park to the shopping centre was straight through the machine tool showroom. So,

Flo set up a trestle table in the middle of the showroom and served free coffee.

'Have a cup of coffee before you start your shopping, luv. Black or white? How does your wife take it?'

And again, when they returned, loaded with shopping. A life-saver, and very hot.

So there was a customer, knowledgeable about machine tools, fed up about shopping, sipping coffee, too hot to drink, in the middle of a machine tool showroom on a Saturday – with his wife.

What does he do? He shows off his knowledge of machine tools to his wife, who never really understood what he did for a living. He demonstrates to her the kind of machines he is responsible for in his job. He demonstrates to her the power and authority he has in his job.

He places orders on Saturday mornings – verbally, and confirms them in writing on the following Monday.

So be different – like Flo Wright.

Focusing the Mind

I knew a salesperson some years ago who was blessed with a wooden leg. Now, not many people would reckon a wooden leg was anything to be blessed with, but, then, not many people could use a wooden leg to make as much money as this salesperson made. He was in a very competitive market that generated regular repeat business. He and a dozen other competitor salespeople fought for the business. He got most of it because of his wooden leg.

Not sympathy business, although if he got any of that he happily took it. No: all he did was use his wooden leg as a Focuser.

When he first met a new prospective customer, he sat with his wooden leg straight out to one side, so that the prospect could see ten centimetres of polished teak between his deliberately short sock and his trouser turn-up. He'd turned down the offer of switching from a polished teak stump to a skin-coloured, lightweight aluminium contraption years before. He knew what he was doing.

The sight of that ten centimetres of polished teak used to hypnotize the customers, he reckoned. They couldn't take their eyes off it.

After a maximum of ten minutes the prospect couldn't help but say: 'Excuse me asking, but is that really wood?'

'Oh yes,' the salesperson would reply, pulling his trouser leg up another 15 centimetres and giving the polished teak a rap with his pen. 'Car accident, years ago.'

A few minutes were then spent talking about the accident, and whether the salesperson suffered when the weather was damp, but the key factor thereafter was that he was never forgotten. Securing the first order was easy. And thereafter, every time the customer said to himself, 'I need to order some more widgets,' the first supplier who came into his mind was 'wooden leg'. So he got most of the on-going business.

I know another young salesperson who, first time he walked into a new prospect's office, overlooked the fact that there were two steps down from the door and fell flat on his face, arms and legs spreadeagled, briefcase and presenter flying into opposite corners of the room. Luckily, he didn't do any damage, to himself or to the prospect's office, only to his pride. The prospect, of course, laughed his socks off. Again, the first order was easy, if only in return for the entertainment provided. But that salesperson gets all the repeat business too, in just as competitive a situation as the guy with the wooden leg.

It's another classic mind jogger. Every time that customer says to himself, 'I must order some more sprunge brackets,' he remembers the guy who fell flat on his face the first time he came into his office.

The salesperson still gets embarrassed and colours up when the customer says to him, laughing: 'Hey, do you remember the first visit you made here ...?', but it doesn't stop him accepting all the business that's going.

It was different for the salesperson who over-emphasized a key point with his fist on the glass-topped desk of the chief buyer, and cracked the glass from front to back. He didn't get the business!

What Would You Do?

A salesperson I know in the financial services business does a lot of work at domestic parlour level, talking to the husband and wife who've been together for 17 years and have never bothered to take out any insurance except on their house, furniture and car. They don't believe in life insurance. It will never happen to them.

This salesperson analysed the domestic Selling situation and pin-pointed the biggest problem. The turning point from total rejection to total reception was getting the couple to think seriously about what they would do if one of them was to go – dead like! Once they'd thought seriously about what they would do, and had realized how long it would take for the money to run out and the difficulties they would have on their own, making ends meet, selling them a policy to cover the situation was easy.

The snag was they didn't *want* to think about it. What the salesperson had to do was find a way of making them think about it, while maintaining total ethics.

After a lot of thought and experimentation, he hit on a winning idea. He had made a beautiful, solid mahogany, brass fittings, about thirty-centimetre-long, miniature coffin. It lived vertically in one side of his briefcase.

In the front room, sitting opposite Gladys and Henry, he'd get to the point of needing both of them to think seriously about what they'd do when one of them bought the farm.

'Just for a couple of minutes,' the salesperson would say to his prospect couple, 'I'd like to get you thinking about something deadly serious.'

He'd reach into his briefcase, bring out the miniature coffin, place it gently and carefully, almost reverently, in the centre of the coffee table between him and the couple, turn to the husband and say:

'God forbid, but let's imagine for a couple of minutes that you are in there.' He puts one finger on the coffin. Then he turns to the wife and asks:

'What would you do?'

There are two or three seconds of pregnant silence and then, every time, the husband starts talking. And the salesperson turns back to him, puts his finger on his lips, points to the coffin and says:

'Shhhh. You're in there.'

Then he turns back to the wife and asks again:

'What would you do?'

After that, the salesperson maintained, the miniature coffin could be put away and it was all plain sailing. A perfectly ethical way of jolting a couple of prospects out of their dream world and making them realize and accept their future problems and responsibilities.

Two Kinds of People

One salesperson who sells investments has a method of tickling his prospects' egos and getting them on to his side. Early on in his presentation, he says to his prospect:

'You know, going through life and meeting as many people as I do, I've found that when it comes to saving money, there are only two kinds of people.'

At this point, the salesperson begins drawing on his A4-size pad. As he draws, he keeps talking. First he draws two circles, like a disjointed pair of spectacles. Then he points to the left-hand circle and says:

'One kind of people tend to spend their income on whatever they need or want to buy, and if they've any left over after that, they might think about saving it, or investing it.'

And while he's saying this, the salesperson is writing '**spend**' in his left-hand circle and then shading in the bottom of the circle, as if it were a quarter full of liquid. Then he points to the right-hand circle and says:

'The other kind of people tend to put some money aside before they start spending, to save or invest.'

And while he's saying this, he shades in the top portion of the right-hand circle and writes '**then spend**' inside the unshaded part of the circle.

Then the salesperson draws an arrow from the bottom of the left-hand circle to the bottom of the right-hand circle.

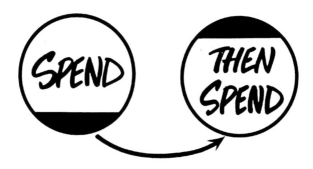

And while he's drawing the arrow, he says:

'And the funny thing is – these kind of people (the left-hand circle) always seem to finish up working for these kind (the right-hand circle).'

Be Better By Being Thorough

Being different is good and is fun. Add being thorough to being different and you have the winning combination.

I'm a great believer in the use of checklists. Why strain the memory or risk forgetting something important. It goes back to 1962 and my second selling job. I was designing and estimating equipment for polishing the edges of glass mirrors. Automated, twenty metres long, very expensive. My company sent me down from Rugby, where I was based, to East London, to measure up for a big one. A whole day of measuring in the prospective customer's works, discussing the project with two of the directors. Everything went very well. I returned to Rugby with sheets of sketches, dimensions, figures, and specifications. But no checklist.

Next day I was at my drawing board, laying out the job to scale. Now, twenty metres is a long piece of tackle to fit into an existing factory, already full of plant and people. Then, as the day and the drawing progressed, I began having this vision. I could see this dirty great vertical stanchion sticking up, floor to roof, in the middle of the factory. Yet I hadn't a single reference to it in my notes and sketches. No, I must be imagining things. I tried to convince myself. It's in some other factory I've visited recently.

But the vision kept coming back. I began sweating. If I carried on in normal sales-office estimating fashion, working to the edict, 'If in doubt, guess!' I knew, with my luck, the twenty-metre-long machine I was responsible for would run straight through the bit of the factory where stood the stanchion. Thank heavens for one thing. I may have been a novice salesperson at that time, but I wasn't a bad engineer, and the edict for engineers is different from the edict for sales-office estimating. The edict for engineers is, 'If in doubt, ask!'.

So I plucked up the courage and telephoned one of the directors I'd spoken with the day before in East London.

'Er ... sorry to bother you, but I need to ask you a question. Have you got a stanchion in the middle of your factory?'

I was really sweating. It sounded such a stupid thing to ask anyone.

'Yes,' the director replied cautiously. 'Why do you ask?'

87

'Well, I seem to have missed it on the notes I took yesterday. Er, have you got a tape measure handy?'
'I might be able to find one.' The director was even more cautious. 'Why?'
'I wonder, would you mind measuring how far your stanchion is from the sides of your factory?'
There was silence for a good 20 seconds. I could hear him breathing. Heavily! Then, 'Ring me back in half an hour!' and he slammed the phone down.
For the next half-hour I was convincing myself I should have made the journey to London again, instead of telephoning. Looking back, it's clear that all I really needed to have had for my visit was a well-thought-out checklist, one of the questions being, 'Is anything likely to get in the way?'.

I'm not alone in my misery. I know a salesperson who relied on a discussion across a desk, rather than taking the trouble to see for himself. He was selling a rather tall piece of equipment. About five metres high, in fact. So he asked the obvious question, 'What's the roof height in your factory?'
The answer, without hesitation, was 'six metres high'.

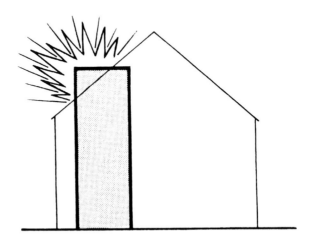

But when the equipment was delivered, the choice he had was either to dig a hole in the concrete floor or bash a hole in the roof, because the roof was pitched and the six metres was the height at the apex. The salesperson's equipment went up against one of the side walls, and there the roof height was only four metres.

It didn't do the slightest bit of good, blaming the customer for the error.

Being thorough comes in all shapes and sizes. My favourite checklist of all is the one which covers the customer's objectives. I developed the example overleaf for a materials handling company, back in 1974.

A company sales engineer used this checklist to broaden the mind of his prospective customer – to open up for him a whole new world. He did this by showing his prospect the Objectives List at an appropriate and early stage in his presentation and saying:

> 'Our products usually enable our customers to achieve seven objectives which, to them, are pretty important. Most of the seven objectives involve saving the customers a considerable amount of money.
>
> I've got the seven objectives listed on this sheet. Can I ask you – which of them are relevant in your case? Which of these seven would your company like to achieve?'

The prospect looked down the list. He'd probably been worrying for some time about how to reduce his non-productive handling time and how to cut his labour costs. He indicated as much to the sales engineer.

But he'd probably never even thought of reducing maintenance costs, gaining space, improving labour relations, throughput, safety Was he going to be interested? You bet.

OBJECTIVES

Customer _____

Date _____

What does the Customer want to do – and why does he want to do it?

Detailed objectives that this Customer wants to achieve (Strike out the sections which do not apply)	Order of Priority
INCREASE PRODUCTION/THROUGHPUT/VEHICLE TURNROUND	
REDUCE HANDLING TIME	
REDUCE LABOUR REQUIREMENT	
REDUCE MAINTENANCE COSTS	
BETTER UTILISATION OF EQUIPMENT	
BETTER UTILISATION OF SPACE	
IMPROVE LABOUR RELATIONS/SAFETY (Union attitude, accident rate, absenteeism, fatigue)	
OTHER FACTORS?	

The minimum number of relevant objectives for each prospective customer, achieved by the sales engineer who used this particular objectives list, was four.

Often, it rose to six. Once the relevant objective had been identified, the salesperson went on to define more precisely what this particular prospective customer wanted to achieve for each relevant section. The precise objectives were written in the spaces provided under each heading.

Then the sales engineer asked his prospect to put the relevant, precisely defined, objectives into priority order. 'Which of these four do you reckon is the most important to you? Which is number one? I'd like to get them in order of priority if you don't mind?'

After that, the selling, and the justification for the purchase, was easy.

How thorough should you be? Well, if you were selling medium to large computers or similar capital equipment where board level sanction and budgets were required, consider this sales checklist from the Japanese Facom Computers organization. I came across it in Australia, and there Facom were beating all comers.

This checklist, headed 'Profile of a Sale', lists the 11 key stages a Facom salesperson is required to go through from the beginning to the end of one potential sale.

PROFILE OF A SALE

1. RESEARCH PROSPECT
    Annual report
    Company structure
    Cross directorships

2. ESTABLISH CONTACTS
    Plan objectives for each call
    Top down or bottom up?

3. MEET DECISION-MAKER AND RECOMMENDER

4. ESTABLISH NEEDS AND WANTS WITH DECISION-MAKER
    Probe for company 5-year plans with decision-maker
    What are the key business decisions of the prospect?
    Who makes these decisions?

5. BASIS OF DECISION
    Unique to FACOM?
    Relevant to decision-maker
    Written down?
    Can FACOM satisfy all points?
    Favourable cost/benefit ratio?

6. FACOM REVIEW
    Review Basis of Decision with Manager and assess %
       chance of obtaining the order

7. RESOURCE ALLOCATION FOR SURVEY

8. SURVEY
    Review findings with prospect middle management
    Have you established all objections?

9. PRESENTATION
    Plan and rehearse

10. PROPOSAL
    Document only what you have sold
    Does it satisfy all the points in the Basis of Decision?
    Sense of Urgency?

11. CLOSE
    Close quickly or find out why not?
    Have you followed the Profile?

That's what I call being thorough.

Using Survey Checklists

How do really good salespeople get all the information and data they need to build effective sales presentations for customers?

By asking the customers for it. (But not the way I did back in 1962!)

The secret is in how the salespeople ask, and the information and data for which they ask.

Really good salespeople think it all out beforehand – and they *don't* rely on their memory. They use properly designed and properly printed checklists, which fit into their A4-size survey pads. (You'll eventually learn to love A4-size survey pads as I do!). Remember:

MEMORY IS WHAT YOU FORGET WITH!

Here are two examples of well thought-out survey checks lists – one for a problem-solving situation involving capital equipment or specialist services; the other for establishing what competition the user is up against.

Survey Checklist – Problem Solving

1. What specifically do you want to achieve?
2. What is the problem costing you?
3. How are you thinking of solving it?
4. Who else is involved in this problem or in finding a solution to it?
5. What would happen if you did nothing?
6. How much money has been allocated to solving this problem?
7. How did you reach this particular figure?
8. When will this money be available?
9. If we can produce a significantly better solution for slightly more than your budget figure, will you consider it?

Survey Checklist – Competitors

1. Which other suppliers are you discussing this problem with?
2. Have you used any of these suppliers before?
3. When are the other quotations due?
4. Who decides which supplier gets the order?
5. Which supplier do you favour at this stage?
6. Why?
7. Does it give you a problem, the fact that you haven't done business with us before?

Be Better By Being Faster

There are some businesses where the first salesperson in, following up an enquiry, gets the order because time is the essence and there is no advantage to the customer in delaying the decision until he's seen another couple of potential suppliers.

Quite often, customers in this situation send out enquiries to several suppliers, all at the same time. Thus, the fastest response gets the business. Half an hour could lose it and I know salespeople who have seen, literally seen, a competitor pick up an order which would have been theirs had they been able to find somewhere to park the car. The answer to being *fastest*, if this is your business, is – *get a mobile telephone or a pager.*

The cost is rubbish if it enables you to pick up orders that otherwise a more agile salesperson would win, simply by being in closer communication with the office. Pagers, which tell you to ring your office fast, can be hired for as little as £2 per month. Mobile phones which can send and receive text messages are incredibly cheap to buy and run. (In this age of high-speed tele- and radio-communications, there are STILL thousands of business managers who deny their salesforces these common-sense, cost-effective selling tools.)

Alternatively, if your area is small and compact and parking your car is your biggest problem, use a bicycle, moped, motorbike or a taxi, keep your phone switched on and ring your office every hour on the hour to keep tabs on those enquiries.

No Reason to Change

The thorniest barrier to progress in Selling! The prospective customer comes out to reception to talk to the salesperson. The salesperson leaps to his feet and extends greetings and thanks for a few minutes of the customer's time. The customer holds up his hands like a traffic cop and says:

'We've been doing business quite satisfactorily with Apex Distributors for seven years now and see absolutely no reason to change – but if you'd like to leave your literature, I'll put it in our suppliers' file.'

The door quite firmly shut – unless, with determination and technique, the salesperson can open it again.

'When you started to use Apex seven years ago, Mr Arnold, what made you choose them as your supplier?'

Mr Arnold has to come up with something. Just hope he remembers! If he mentions two or three factors that caused them to pick Apex, or to switch to Apex from another supplier:

'Are these factors still the same ones today?'

If Mr Arnold says, 'Yes', then great. If he says 'No':

'How have they changed? What are your criteria for ordering for the foreseeable future? Can I get it down on my survey pad?'

Then the salesperson plays his ace:

'It's a fact the world over, Mr Arnold, that 92 per cent of all the products in use today have been invented, introduced or refined into their present form within the last ten years. 'So if you're still using something that you started using seven years ago, you may be perfectly happy with it, but there's a good chance that by now there will be something better available. Certainly, in our particular business there have been many developments these past few years.
'Shouldn't you take ten minutes to find out for sure that you're still getting best value for your money, because quite frankly, I don't think you can be?'

Be Better By Being Honest

A rich businessman accosted a beautiful blonde at a cocktail party.

> 'For a thousand pounds, will you sleep with me tonight?'
> 'You bet,' she replied, looking him straight in the eye.
> 'For five pounds will you sleep with me tonight?'
> 'What?' she exclaimed. 'You must be joking. What kind of a girl do you think I am?'
> 'We've established what kind of girl you are, my dear,' the businessman smiled. 'All we have to do is decide the price.'

The very mention of bribery and corruption in business, and of over-lavish entertainment and company yachts or grouse shoots, invariably sends shudders through any organization since John Poulson and Watergate and Lockheed blew the *status quo* through the roof.

But, there is still a lot of it about and it comes in all shapes and sizes. The average salesperson probably comes up against it every day. Maybe he doesn't recognize the fact but it's there all the same. The story preceding this paragraph illustrates the basic factor in bribery and corruption. It takes *two* people to make it happen. Two basically dishonest people – a buyer and a salesperson. And either one can start the ball rolling.

Let's consider a typical situation when a dishonest buyer and a dishonest salesperson get together. The buyer encourages and accepts a gift from the salesperson for favours above and beyond his duty of getting the best deal for his company. In other words, in exchange for the gift – which might be cash in the back pocket, membership of some exotic club, a free holiday, his house painted, a car at a bargain price or a thousand other things – he buys from a supplier who does not give him best value for money.

Having accepted the gift and placed the order, this buyer is stuck with this salesperson. He buys again and again. He has to. He cannot stop doing business with the salesperson for fear that his indiscretion will be leaked to his management – or worse, to the local newspapers.

The cleverest dishonest buyers manage, however, to cover

themselves by still making sure they get the best deals for their companies. The dishonest salesperson's competitor comes up with a lower price. The buyer contacts his supplier straight away and says:

'George, Apex Distributors have offered me grade B Widgets at five per cent less than your current price. You'll have to match it, or my directors will soon find out.'

So the dishonest salesperson either drops his price and keeps the business, or lets the dishonest buyer off the hook. If he aims to keep the business at all costs, two years of these tactics and he'll be lucky if he has any profit left at all. And this is business he is buying!

Of course, the dishonest buyer's directors will soon find out if he doesn't make sure he keeps on getting the best possible deals for his company. The dishonest salesperson's competitors will do their very best to bring the problem to the directors' attention. What they'd like to see is the dishonest buyer replaced by someone with whom they can do business.

Faced with this, the less astute dishonest buyers don't last very long. But most of them leave before they're pushed.

Tactics for Beating the Bribers

If the deal you have to offer is the same or only marginally better than the deal the dishonest buyer is getting from the competitor he is buying from, you are going to have big problems. Let's face it, you're going to have big problems with *honest* buyers if you've nothing extra to offer.

You've got you, of course. You'll look after them better. You'll see that they get the best possible attention from your company's service engineers. You give them your home telephone number and tell them they can contact you at any time, any evening, over the weekend if they need anything.

And you've got Second Source. They've got all their eggs in one basket. Dumb dishonest buyers invariably have.

'What would happen, Mr Thick, if Apex Distributors had a fire, or a strike, or went bust, and suddenly, without warning, couldn't supply you?

'How long would it take you to open an account with another supplier and to get things back to normal supply levels? Even two weeks would give you big problems, wouldn't it?

'If you were already buying, say, twenty per cent of your widgets from a second source supplier, it would be so much easier for you to pick up the phone and get the second supplier to increase supplies fast, wouldn't it?

And twenty per cent wouldn't hurt your relationship with your main supplier, would it? You're only taking out some insurance and they must understand the wisdom and the logic of that.'

Help him get himself just a little bit off the hook, and once you've established a toe-hold ...

If you *do* have a significantly better deal to offer a customer who is currently buying from one of your competitors and you come up against inexplicable obstacles which make you wonder if you are up against a dishonest buyer – test the water with the most powerful question in Selling:

'Mr Thin, it seems to me that the deal we are offering you is significantly better than you're getting now from Dodgers in at least four ways, including price and quality.

Can I ask you a straight question? Just what do we have to do to get you to buy from us?'

If he's really dumb, he might suggest that you double what he's getting from Dodgers. Then you just pass the problem up the line to your directors and let them deal with it. More likely, he'll break out in a sweat, keep hedging and avoid committing himself. If he does this, you can be 99 per cent certain you've got one of them.

You now have two courses of action, either of which you can take, or both, one after the other.

Course One

You brief your sales director on the situation. You establish with the dishonest buyer or with someone else in his company some days when it is certain he won't be in his office. Your sales director pays a visit, out of the blue, without an appointment. He asks for a few minutes of the dishonest buyer's time. He's told the buyer is not in today. He asks to see the buyer's superior. Because he's a sales director, he stands a good chance of getting face-to-face. In ten minutes, the significantly better deal and the inexplicable obstructions have been discussed. 'How do we get your business?' your sales director asks.

The day the dishonest buyer gets back to his office, your phone rings. 'What the hell's going on?' the buyer rants. 'Your sales director's been in to see my boss, behind my back. I take a bloody dim view of that!'

'Good heavens,' you exclaim. 'I don't know anything about this. Look, give me half an hour to find out what's going on and I'll ring you back.'

You make yourself useful doing other things for half an hour, then you ring the dishonest buyer back.

'I've spoken to my sales director. Given him quite a rocket, actually. It's all quite innocent, really. He was in your area yesterday, and found he had an hour to spare because another meeting ran shorter than scheduled. He knew we had a deal under discussion so he popped in to see you. When he found you were out he asked if anyone else was available and your boss was, so they had a chat. He's ever so choked at annoying you so much. He's asked me to fix a date and time with you for him to call in to see you, so that he can apologise personally. Can you give me a couple of convenient dates in the next week?'

If that doesn't prise the business loose, then try Course Two.

Course Two

The problem, the action taken so far, the suspicions, the details of the better deal, have all been passed upstairs to your managing director.

Your managing director telephones the dishonest buyer's

managing director and invites him to lunch. Over lunch, the better deal is explained. Your managing director is puzzled why his guest's company is apparently not interested. His suspicions are discussed.

His guest assures him he will look into the matter as soon as he gets back to the fort. They relax over coffee and brandy.

A few days later, you will either be asked by a very frigid buyer to call and discuss future supplies, or you will continue making regular, but more fruitful, calls, on the *new* buyer.

But only managing directors can carry through Course Two.

Plot and Counter-Plot

A company in the business equipment field – let's call it Snooks – was seeking to interest a public corporation in a new system for processing mail. The company had one competitor and this competitor was also seeking to interest the public corporation in a similar mail processing system. We'll call the competitor Bloggs.

The Political and Union hierarchy of the public corporation dictated that the corporation's own design and development department should issue drawings and specifications for any new scheme intended for the corporation. Thus, drawings and specifications were duly issued to both Snooks and Bloggs for prototype equipment so that the viability and efficiency of the proposed system could be thoroughly tested before the big commitment was made. The prototypes were to be supplied at the supplier's cost – to be recovered in the subsequent big order.

Snooks, on examining the corporation's drawings and specifications, was alarmed to find that the design was identical to the Bloggs standard equipment. Obviously, someone had gained an inside advantage.

Snooks, knowing that its equipment was superior to Bloggs in a number of respects, devised a plan to deal with this unfair advantage. It knew that when it came to the maintenance of the new system, the public corporation would spend far more money operating the Bloggs equipment than it would operating the Snooks equipment.

Comparison figures, case histories from other customers, graphs, photographs and proposals were put together fast and Snooks' sales team fixed an appointment to talk to the public corporation's maintenance department. Snooks knew that it was highly unlikely that maintenance was ever consulted about new systems until after the installations were completed. That kind of corporation operated on the 'warring tribes' concept.

Snooks' team pointed out to the maintenance people how a few minor changes to the corporation's designs and specifications could radically improve maintenance's part in the future operation of the system. The team was thanked profusely for bringing the matter to maintenance's attention. Yes, they'd certainly take immediate action to get the designs amended. (It wasn't every day they found such a golden opportunity to make the design and development boys suffer!)

Within a few days, Snooks received a letter from the purchasing department of the corporation, asking for all work to stop on the prototype, as changes had had to be made and new drawings and specifications were on their way.

Phase one completed. At least the new drawings and specifications gave Snooks a sporting chance. But the advantage still had to be with Bloggs, because of the obvious close ties they had with someone in the corporation, and because, like most such public corporations, when it came to the tender for the big system, the order would probably still go to the lowest bidder. So Snooks set up a subtle trap.

The Snooks prototype was duly delivered. The usual delivery note accompanied the equipment but unfortunately someone made the mistake of typing on to the delivery note the price of the equipment. The very next day, one of Snooks' salespeople was calling at the corporation's goods inwards depot, rather sheepishly explaining to the clerk that yesterday's delivery note for the prototype equipment had been sent in error and could he exchange it for the correct one.

Two hours and several departments later, the salesperson emerged triumphant, clutching the first delivery note to his breast. But not before, Snooks figured, it had been photocopied a few times and had reached the corporation executive who was in close touch with Bloggs.

The Snooks and the Bloggs prototype equipment both passed all their tests. Formal tenders were submitted in sealed envelopes, in accordance with the corporation's tendering rules, for several hundred of the production versions of the prototype.

Several weeks after Snooks won the order, they established that the price tendered by Bloggs was exactly £100 per unit less than the price that had been typed in error on their prototype's delivery note.

But, of course, the delivery note price had absolutely nothing to do with Snooks' tender price. In fact, the price on the delivery note was considerably higher.

Big Mouth!

There used to be a well known quality restaurant frequented by most of the South Midlands business community. During lunchtimes, in particular, it was normally always full of pairs, trios and quartets, busy discussing business.

A small local engineering firm rose rapidly in prominence, servicing the motor manufacturers in the Coventry area. It became busier and busier, took on more and more staff, and its monthly account at the aforementioned restaurant grew in direct proportion.

Almost every lunchtime, and quite a few evenings, the principal director of the engineering firm was at the restaurant, entertaining customers and potential customers. The booze element of the daily bill often exceeded the food element.

The principal director wasn't very bright. He had a rather loud voice, which became even louder when lubricated. He was also something of a braggart. Other customers in the restaurant had no difficulty listening to his business discussions, even from across the room. The one where he was offering the all-expenses-paid holiday in Italy was particularly interesting. It didn't take long for every regular customer of the restaurant to know in detail how the engineering firm was getting its business.

What the director hadn't bothered to consider (I've said he wasn't very bright), was that the customers of that restaurant ranged all the way up the business hierarchy of the motor industry. The chief executive of one manufacturer was a regular diner, as were the directors and senior executives of most major component suppliers, plus local accountants, solicitors, and estate agents. Socially or through business contacts, the word of what was going on filtered through to the powers-that-be.

Nothing drastic was done, either to the director of the engineering firm or to his main customer contacts. The customer contacts were simply moved to other responsibilities within the motor manufacturers, and eighty per cent of the business going in the direction of the engineering firm stopped overnight.

That the moves were planned is not in any doubt. The restaurant was warned six weeks before to make sure the engineering firm paid all its outstanding accounts by the end of the month, and not to extend any credit whatsoever thereafter.

Our stand at a trade exhibition gives us an opportunity
to get at all our competitors' customers.

But it also gives all our competitors an opportunity
to get at our customers.

So this is a game we simply must be best at,
or we shouldn't do it at all.

Chapter 5

How to Win in the Exhibition Arena

There is still nothing to compare with a stand at a trade exhibition for launching a business and its products or services towards new customers, new contacts and new markets. But success at an exhibition depends on the stand itself being properly designed, the products or services properly displayed, the stand-manning staff performing properly, and the enquiries being logged properly.

Unfortunately, ninety per cent of businesses that exhibit still get at least two of these four provisos wrong – and pour their exhibition budget money down the drain.

This is why quite a few past exhibitors have been heard to comment unfavourably about the 'sport'. A recent survey quoted exhibitors as saying things like, 'Stand space costs £150 a square metre, more than five times the cost of a first-class hotel, but without bed, bath, loo and colour TV. The stand itself costs about the same again', and, 'I'd rather increase coverage by other means without shows. Costs are becoming prohibitive', and, 'In no other activity do managers leave themselves so exposed'.

But the exhibition business is booming – and likely to continue to boom. Most exhibition centres are booked for years ahead. So why are exhibitions good for some businesses and bad for others?

It's a trick question, of course. The answer is that exhibitions should be good for every kind of business. But the approach to exhibiting within the business and the way an exhibition cuts right across all departmental boundaries can give senior executives a jaundiced opinion of this key element in sales promotion.

One big problem is that businesses tend to look at the cost of an exhibition stand in isolation. They rarely compare the costs with alternative ways to generate the same amount of orders, or enquiries.

Let me give you an example. If you were head of a machine tool manufacturing or distributing business, and I walked into your office one day and told you I could supply you with a list of names and addresses of people who have already shown an interest in buying your machine tools, what would you say?

I'll bet your first question would be 'How much?'

If I replied, '£60 per name and address', I'd stand a good chance of getting thrown out on my ear.

But consider the nature of the machine tool business. You have a salesforce out there, making most of their calls on prospective customers, rather than existing customers – because machine tools is essentially a 'one-off' business, and highly competitive. You're up against forty or more competitors on every sales territory.

Your salesforce makes a lot of cold canvass calls, without the benefit (so far) of the techniques we discussed in Chapter 2. On average, for every ten cold canvass calls, the salesforce gets face-to-face with one possible prospect – a 'warm one'. But you know that a call, any kind of call, costs £60 to make. That's a simple piece of arithmetic – total cost of the salesforce divided by the number of calls made, for any given period of time.

So one 'warm one' costs £600 if you let your salesforce handle the job. And you threw me out on my ear when I offered you a list of warm ones for a tenth of the cost.

That's how people often look at the cost of exhibiting.

I used this example because I have been involved, as a consultant, in the planning and manning of several exhibition stands at the International Machine Tool Exhibition and other major shows.

The budget, not including the cost of the machines on display, was £120,000. Over the duration of the Exhibition, the stand-manning staff *sold* all the machines on the stand and logged the names and addresses of more than 1,200 people they hitherto didn't know existed, who set foot on the stand and showed an interest in the machines.

If we assume that the sale of the actual machines on display covered the labour costs of all the staff involved on the stand, we're left with 1,200 'warm ones' and a cost of £120,000 for being there.

That's £100 per logged name and address!

Whatever your business, this is the way you should cost out the viability of the exhibitions in which you consider participating.

Why Are You Exhibiting?

Are you aiming to increase your market share? Maintain your market share? Recover your past market share?

Does your market penetration need to spread, go deeper, or be re-directed? Are you seeking to probe into a new market, explore the unknown, or infiltrate a competitor's market with malice aforethought?

Are you seeking to promote to your customers and potential customers new applications for your products, new features and benefits of your products, improved quality, longer life, new versatility, new design, colour, shape?

Are you aiming to show off products or services that are new to the Industry the Exhibition caters for, or new to the markets for which you cater?

Are you aiming to introduce new trademarks or brand names or to pioneer 'ahead-of-its-time' new technology?

Or are you just considering a stand because you have an uneasy feeling that because the competition is going to be there, you ought to be there?

Whatever the reason, you'd better be sure of it – and it had better be a good, valid reason – before you begin planning the event.

Here is another good reason for exhibiting. It is a table of statistics from Hugh Buckner's *How British Industry Buys* and concerns how the various executives in a customer company acquire information on products and services they need to buy.

In industry, personnel with these functions (right) consider, in the percentages shown, the factors (below) to be amongst the two most important when obtaining information on products	Board (general management)	Operating management	Production engineering	Design and development engineering	Maintenance engineering	Research	Buying	Finance	Sales	Others
Catalogues	39	36	45	64	34	64	52	32	44	76
Direct mail	12	9	14	6	31	21	23	14	5	27
Salespersons' visits	66	61	60	67	78	64	64	60	73	40
Advertisements in trade press	14	32	28	22	21	15	12	23	24	24
Exhibitions	15	17	11	11	47	15	9	19	14	12
Demonstrations by manufacturers	50	41	35	26	37	21	37	38	45	22
Other	6	4	6				5	5	35	

The Exhibition Budget

When it comes to putting together a budget for an exhibition stand, the 'ostrich complex' normally prevails. Items that should be included in the exhibition budget are hived off and buried elsewhere, to reduce apparent expenditure. Tackle the budgeting as if you were presenting a Proposal to a prospective customer: include cost/benefit ratios, objectives, recommendations for achieving the objectives, financial justification, even guarantees and third-party references (past successful exhibitors and ABC past-attendance figures).

Here's a list of most of the items that should be included in your exhibition budget (use the blank space for your figures):

The Stand

1. Stand space
2. Stand design
3. Furniture and fittings
   Functional
   Protective
   For decoration
4. Exhibits
   Main items
   Auxiliary equipment
   Sign writing
5. Publicity display equipment
6. Stand transport charges
   To exhibition
   From exhibition
   Mechanical handling
   Packing
7. Construction charges
   Erection
   Dismantling
   Maintenance
   Sundry labour

8. Other costs
    Services
    Communication
    Insurance
    Entertainment
    Clerical aids
    Security
    Safety
    Cleaning
    Waste disposal
    Repairs
    Consumables

The Staff

1. Your own staff's salaries
2. Other staff's salaries
    Demonstrators
    Hostesses
    Interpreters
    Others
3. Expenses
    Travel (to, from, at)
    Hotel
    Living
    Equipment, clothing

Promotion

1. Advertising and PR
    Before
    During
    After
2. Sales and technical literature
3. Other publicity materials
4. Give-aways
5. Catalogue entry and advertising

The 'Hilton' Rule

Conrad Hilton, founder of the world-famous hotel chain, claims there are only three factors that guarantee the success of a hotel:

Position, position and position!

So it is with an exhibition stand. If you're stuck in some minor side gangway in the annex, you'll only attract a small fraction of the number of visitors who actually attend the exhibition. It's like advertising in the wrong publication. Not enough of your market notices your advertisement!

This means your planning has to begin early, so that you have the pick of the prime stand space (assuming, of course, you can afford the prime space). Opposite the main entrance; in full view of the stairs leading from one main hall to another; next to the restaurant or, better still, the bar; adjacent to the toilets – these are normally the best positions.

You have yet another problem. More and more exhibition organizers are insisting that you conform to the standard shell scheme for overall stand design. This tends to produce overall monotony and a very flat top-surface view if you pick a high vantage point and assume the role of a prospective customer, looking out over the entire exhibition hall, trying to pick out your stand. A good stand designer can turn this to advantage, giving you a slightly higher 'focal point', even by cheating a little, and creating 'a focus of interest in a desert of imagination', for your stand design in general.

But don't let the designer get carried away. The object of the exercise is to display and sell your products or services, not his creativity. Make sure the stand itself doesn't look more attractive than the products being displayed, otherwise you'll find yourself selling exhibition stands!

Use a professional designer and stand building organizer, because your stand *must* look professional, not as if it's been cobbled together at the last minute by the sales department, who'd forgotten until last week that the exhibition was even taking place. Never, never, never use existing display units from your front offices or factory. Your stand needs to be an integrated whole, not a series of isolated, disjointed, second-hand bits and pieces. The competition will love it, but your customers and your salesforce will despise it. Better not to be there at all.

The Barriers

Your objective, in being there, is to attract as many people on to your stand as you can during the show (isn't it?). What you do with them once you've got them on to your stand we'll discuss later.

The incredible thing is, how many exhibitors seem deliberately to make it as difficult as possible for casual prospects to walk on to their stands. They build barriers around the stand, They restrict the single entrance and exit to one metre maximum, and position a salesperson in the centre of the entrance, his feet ten centimetres over the edge, arms folded, and a 'ready-to-repel-boarders' expression on his gloomy face. (Actually, it's last night's booze-up that's making his head and his feet ache!)

Casual prospects (and this describes the majority of people you're trying to catch) won't come near your stand unless they can see clearly as they approach that they can easily walk on – and easily walk off again without being captured. That's their subconscious talking, and it's a very powerful argument.

So make sure your stand designer bears this firmly in mind.

My prize for barrier building goes to a scaffolding firm at the Materials Handling Exhibition a few years ago. They'd given the job of designing the stand to one of their own draughtsmen with the instructions, 'Build as much of the product into the design as you can'.

The result was a towering mass of scaffolding, within which was the discussion platform and chairs, tables, etc. – *one and a half metres off the ground*. Worse than that, the only access to and from the discussion platform was one set of portable steps, stores variety. The 'gallows steps' deterrent. No casual potential customers will journey up a set of steps, especially to reach a discussion area immediately

112

beneath several tons of scaffolding.

Over five days, I don't think that company logged a single name and address of anyone who wasn't already a customer.

Be open. Be welcoming. Look friendly. No implied threats to life or limb.

Signs and Colours

Here are a few specifications, because I know from experience they are hard to find elsewhere.

The signs you use on your stand need to be read clearly from a number of different distances, ranging from the other side of the hall, 'Ah! There they are, over there!', to a couple of feet away, 'That's interesting. I didn't know UWC's widget crusher would do that'.

So the *size* of your lettering needs to be appropriate to the purpose of the sign itself. Here are the minimum sizes and distances for clear reading:

6 metres away – lettering 5 centimetres high (minimum)
15 metres away – lettering 7.5 centimetres high (minimum)
20 metres away – lettering 10 centimetres high (minimum)
30 metres away – lettering 13 centimetres high (minimum)
over 30 metres away – lettering 15 centimetres high (minimum)

If you use polystyrene letters, fire regulations now dictate it must be self-extinguishing grade.

On colour, don't ever get hooked on just your house colour; you'll ruin your stand if you do. Use colours to accentuate your product or service displays. Here's another list of colour 'feelings':

Blue is cold
Red is warm
Green is soothing (unless it's acid or 'puke'!)
White is clinical
Yellow is fresh

Models

I'm not going to talk about the female variety, who are rarely properly briefed to do anything useful except look gorgeous and pacify complainers. I want to say a few words about what you can do if you haven't any products to display, because you sell a service.

One such company I can use as an example is Knight Wegenstein Ltd, consultants to the foundry industry. At every Foundry Exhibition, you'll find KW at the bottom of the steps leading from Hall 5 into Hall 4 at the National Exhibition Centre, a huge yellow KW inverted triangle on the front of their stand, acting as a superb focal point to attract the casual visitor.

On the stand itself is an intricate table-top model of an automated foundry, under a sheet of thick perspex. No one can resist a good model. Referring to aspects of the model foundry, KW's stand staff can discuss any aspect of their consultancy services.

I've seen lifting-gear specialists with models of building sites full of tower cranes with which the visitors can play games. I've seen testing laboratories with flight simulators and racing cars on their stands as focal points. I've even seen a cleaning-services company with a stand consisting of an elaborate model railway.

My favourite services stand didn't use a model. It designed the stand completely as a café. Complete with rows of little square tables covered with chintzy tablecloths, a tea counter with polished tea urns, and half a dozen waitresses. The stand in question was at the Hanover Fair. The company actually *cleaned* the Hanover Fair, and about half the factories and offices in West Germany. Every visitor to the café was a valid potential customer. Great stuff. Scalding hot tea and coffee. Once visitors had sat down and accepted a cup, they were locked in there for a minimum ten minutes – the time it took for their drink to cool down enough to touch their lips!.

No Telephones

Why do you want telephones on an exhibition stand? No one from the works should be allowed to contact the stand staff during exhibition opening hours and the stand staff certainly shouldn't want to contact anyone outside while they are on duty. When they're off-duty they can find a telephone somewhere else or use the one in your hospitality suite (next subject).

If the telephone is on the specification only because the Chairman likes to use it on the day he visits the stand, take it off the spec. Take his chair and desk away too!

Mobile phones have taken the place of fixed phones nowadays – but beware the steel-framed exhibition hall screening and the fact that hundreds of mobiles are trying to access the same local receiving station at the same time – like Friday evening, getting out of London and trying to ring home with your ETA.

Hospitality and Hospitality Suites

During the planning stages you should decide whether to allow boozing on your stand, or to keep it dry and rent a hospitality suite or room, adjacent to the exhibition hall.

That's what we did at one Machine Tool Exhibition, long reputed to be 'the wettest show on earth!' No drinks of any kind on the stand, no personal belongings, no off-duty stand staff, no literature, no telephone. Just business.

Any existing customer who walked on to the stand, unless he'd come to see something in particular, was whisked away ASAP to the hospitality suite by his local sales engineer or by one of our hospitality girls (from the Company's sales office, plus two wives of directors). There he could booze in private, out of sight and reach of our competitors at the show. We wooed lots of their customers in that suite and the competitors didn't know a thing about it!

Any existing customer who'd come to the stand to lodge a complaint was in the hospitality suite so fast, his feet hardly touched the ground. The last place you need a complaining customer is publicly in the middle of your exhibition stand.

Any potential customer who requested literature was taken to the hospitality suite for a drink, his name and address and requirements written down by the girl on the literature desk in the suite. An address label would be printed out on her word processor there and then and a large envelope of literature was in the post that very night, to be on his desk waiting for him when he got back to his office. You don't want to carry literature around for the rest of the day, Sir. Let me take your name, address and particulars and we'll get it in the post tonight to your office' (pointing to word processor).

While I'm on the subject of hospitality, let's consider the kind of hospitality you tend to give your existing customers.

At an exhibition, you have an opportunity to show your gratitude for past business placed, with champagne or something suitable. But you don't necessarily want to go splashing champagne around for the casual punters and the hangers on. Lagers, gin and tonics, teas, coffees, crisps and peanuts will normally do for these people. So how do you separate the two?

You can't totally. But you can go at least halfway – and even halfway will result in a big saving in cases of champagne.

Select one day of the show and invite all your existing customers to your stand on that day, and to one of a series of celebrations held that day in your hospitality suite. Not all your customers will be able to attend that day, but a sufficient number will to make a considerable saving for the rest of the show.

Your top brass always attend on this day, of course. It's the existing customers they need to talk to.

Do this, and you'll find the rest of the days will be relatively clear of existing customers (whom you can call on any old time – you know who and where they are), so that you can concentrate more fully on capturing the potential customers and your competitors' customers.

Just a note here about private 'At Home' exhibitions, where you invite selected customers and prospective customers to your own show in your own showroom. Take two days for the event and invite your customers on one day and your prospects on the other. Same thing then applies for the booze.

It Will Start – Whether You Are Ready Or Not!

Early on in the planning stages, your exhibition stand team should have sat through the Video Arts Ltd training video, *It'll be Okay on the Day*. Each member of the team should also be in possession of the Video Arts/Andry Montgomery Group booklet, 'What every exhibitor ought to know', full of checklists for both planning and manning an exhibition stand.

Later on in the process you should be showing the stand-manning team the second Video Arts video, *How Not to Exhibit Yourself!* which is referred to in the booklet.

One of the checklists in this booklet is intended to help you make sure your that stand is ready for the opening of the show. The top ten rules of project management are as follows:

1. Agree objectives.
2. Establish command.
3. Establish responsibilities.
4. Plan all dates backwards from opening day.
5. Every manager must have his own calendar.
6. Fix key meetings a long way in advance.
7. Circulate information religiously.
8. Chase progress relentlessly.
9. Check budgets regularly.
10. Resist afterthoughts ruthlessly.

(If you're currently contemplating a stand at a major show, nine months ahead, I hate to tell you, but you should have begun the planning three months ago!)

If *you* are the fortunate person to have been designated 'Stand Manager', with the responsibilities of the Captain of a ship, even over the chairman, let us move on to those hectic few days before the opening of the show, when you and your team are working 14 hours a day in the exhibition hall, frantically trying to get everything ready for D-day.

What You Can Do and What You Can't Do

If you've been there before, you'll doubtless know the rules – written and unwritten! Don't try to beat the system. If you do, all the exhibition construction labour, the carpenters, the painters, the electricians, the furniture contractors, the carpet layers, the flower people, will down tools in a flash and every other exhibitor at the show will be blaming *you*.

You can 'dress' your own stand, which implies handling anything that is free standing. You can do your own fetching and carrying – they're not proud! But *no tools*. Don't even mend a fuse.

If you use your own workforce to help with the free-standing exhibits, the positioning of the products, the testing and running of anything that's going to actually perform during the show, or the erection of partitions, the workers must belong to the right Unions.

Most major exhibition halls publish a comprehensive document on what you can do and what you can't. Don't rely on just the information you get from the exhibition organizer – he just hires the hall. If in doubt, go direct to source for the full facts.

A hot tip from me. If you want your stand finished *first*, not last, first thing you do when you get to the exhibition hall is you make contact with the Union organizer or, better still, the Area Convenor, if there's such a body on site.

'My name's John Fenton, UWC, stand number 76 in Hall 4. I'm responsible for the stand. Just thought I'd say hello and find out if there is anything I should know, or can tell you, so that we get the stand finished with plenty of time to spare.

Who are your people I should talk to for lighting and for final sign touching up?

Where do I make contact with them?

Who should I talk to if we encounter any problems?'

He'll get the message. And the tip when the job's completed.

Any bits and pieces you need, extra to the original agreed list with the labour force, you pay 50 per cent of the cash up front, and 50 per cent when the job's done. It's the only way – otherwise you'll stay at the bottom of the list. Don't forget, there's a lot of other stand managers, all trying to be first to finish.

Have at least £1,000 in cash on you if you're stand manager for a major show in Britain. I don't know what the going rate is for any other country – but I do know there is one.

Don't Forget the Excitement

One final point before we move on to how to win during the exhibition itself.

Exhibitions should be exciting. Your stand should be exciting. Your stand staff should catch the mood of the show, because it is 'Show Business'.

If your stand design is drab, lacking in colour and movement and *life*, your stand staff will perform likewise.

Staffing the Stand

Staffing a stand at a trade exhibition is an incredibly tiring occupation, both physically and mentally. Bear one fact of life very clearly in mind – the guards outside Buckingham Palace are changed every two hours, and they just have to stand there!

Don't expect anyone to be able to put in an eight-hour day, for five days, on an exhibition stand *and* be sharp, professional, and able to take advantage of every opportunity that presents itself. It can't be done.

You'll need a rota system. Two hours on and two hours off. And by 'off' I mean off and away from the stand, not lounging about taking up very expensive selling space. (The benefits of a hospitality suite again!) You need enough stand staff to make the rota system work, you need a good stand manager who can make the discipline of running a successful stand stick, and you need a good deputy stand manager, just in case of accidents. Then you need the appropriate number of auxilliary stand staff – for reception, clerical duties, technical for demonstrations, specialists and top brass, linguists if it is an International show and you're trying to capture export business.

Don't sort this out *ad hoc*. Plan it well in advance.

If you have any choice in the selection of stand-manning staff, here is a checklist you might find useful. Think about each individual on each of the eight factors, plus sub-factors, before deciding yes or no. If you yourself are on the short list, take it personally and see if you can measure up positively to all eight.

1. Educational background
   General
   Technical
   Special
   Languages
2. Training
   What has been given?
   What is its relevance to the exhibition?
3. Exhibition experience
   Types attended

Venues – home/overseas
Duties carried out
4. Contacts
   In location – home/overseas customers
   Other exhibitors
   Exhibition authorities
5. Personality
   Behaviour
   Appearance
   Self-confidence
   General attitude
   What is it?
6. Attitude to stand duty
7. Attitude to 'exhibitions'

A few comments about this checklist:

On **Personality** – you need happy people; people who look smart, behave professionally, won't frighten the casual visitors. Try to avoid anyone whose facial characteristics make them look bad-tempered, gruesome, aggressive or frightening. (I employed a guy once who was so gaunt his face looked like a skeleton with skin in harsh light. I never put him on stand duty.)

On **General Attitude** – you need the 'Company' person, rather than the loner. Choose the people who have the interests of the business at heart.

On **Attitude to Stand Duty** – you're looking for the people who see the task of manning an exhibition stand as exciting (for the right reasons) rather than those who consider it a chore.

On **Attitude to 'Exhibitions'** – you're looking for those 'Company' people who see the exhibition as something that will clearly do the business some good, who understand the things that can be achieved and maybe some of the things that can't!

The rest of this chapter is a true-life story of one business aiming to beat its competitors comprehensively in the exhibition arena. Use this example as a blueprint for your next show.

D-Day Minus 7

Today, seven days before the exhibition opens, the whole manning team attended a **briefing**. It was thorough, thank goodness, lasting all morning. Plenty of time and opportunity for questions.

The main objectives of being at the exhibition were stated, examined, questioned and agreed. Don't often see a unanimous vote in this Company, but we got one here.

Then we went through each of the products we'll be having on the stand, its position, what key benefits we'll need to stress to visitors, the back-up literature for each. The boss had a giant drawing of the stand plan on one wall and a model of the complete stand and exhibits which we could all walk round and view from all approach directions. These helped a lot.

We were made to write down the three main objectives for all the stand-manning staff:

- To make direct sales.
- To set up appointments for future calls.
- To get the names and addresses and interests of every person who sets foot on our stand during the show whom we hitherto didn't know

Samples of the exhibition enquiry forms we would be using were handed round and a couple of role-plays were conducted to test procedure for bugs and gremlins. Another unanimous vote.

The boss appointed the Stand Manager and his deputy and publicly, in front of the whole team, delegated his own authority to the Stand Manager for the duration of the show. I can still hear the boss's words:

'Jim Thomas has the same authority next week as the captain of a ship. His ship will be this exhibition stand. If he needs to throw you overboard, set you adrift on a cutting-out or foraging expedition or press gang more hands, that's what he'll do, and he'll speak with my voice. Believe it.

If I get in the way, he has the authority to throw me overboard,

The discipline on our stand next week is going to help us flatten the competition, steal a lot of their customers, and keep them well away from our customers.

I look to you all to give Jim 100 per cent support.'

Then we discussed stand security, competitive tactics during the show, procedures for handing in our enquiries twice a day – once at 1pm and again at close of business – and the diary for special visitors.

Rotas were drawn up and agreed. Hotel reservations were verified. Touch wood, no one looked like going sick or getting married or arrested next week.

The girls who will be handling the hospitality suite and the literature stocks went through their procedures, Another two role-plays, one for a drunken complainer. Lots of fun, but everyone got the message.

The boss did his usual thing about getting to bed reasonably early each night. The discussion on how he defined 'reasonably' lasted twenty minutes. When will some of these people grow up?

This time, we didn't get a unanimous vote, but the majority, for no later than midnight, was considerable. And the boss had the Ace anyway – the exhibition party was on the LAST night, with no early-to-bed stipulation and the opportunity of a lie-in the next morning (clear hotel rooms by 12 noon and pay bill on departure). But if anyone reported unfit for duty at 8.30 any morning during the show, or couldn't pass the walk-the-white-line test, the party would be cancelled.

Any other activities, business or pleasure, during the show, were banned for every member of the manning team.

Finally we discussed the competitions we were participating in during the show and tactics for demoralizing our competitors. Exhibitor's badges, tickets and car parking passes were allocated.

This is really going to be a great exhibition. I can feel it already.

D-Day Minus 1

The one thing about the day before an exhibition opens is that, except for the stand builders' vehicles, you can park easily. So for the familiarization briefing, everyone arrived punctually.

Jim Thomas, as Stand Manager, briefed us all on the stand layout. He showed us where the electrical switchboard was sited, where the emergency telephone was locked away (one key only, and Jim's got it), the best route to our hospitality suite so as to avoid our competitors' stands, where we keep our personal belongings, visitors' belongings, the booze and the food in the hospitality suite.

Then we did a conducted tour of the exhibition hall to establish the geography of the place, where the telephones, toilets, bars, restaurants, press office, first aid, lost property and lifts were situated. If we'd had time, I reckon Jim would have organized an army-style survival test.

Jolly useful couple of hours, though. I'll cut a good half hour off my journey each day as a result. Didn't realise there were so many short cuts and easier ways of getting from A to B and back again.

D-Day

Well, everything is ready on time. The Royals are opening the exhibition. The visitors are starting to stream in. I feel great. I know what I have to do. I'm armed and ready with survey pad, exhibition enquiry form and a spare in my pocket. Everything's been tested and proved to be working. All I've got to do is get the first order today and win that bottle of champagne (which I will receive *next* week!)

Seeing that Video Arts film again last night was a good final recap. *How Not to Exhibit Yourself!* Ha. Won't see us making any of those mistakes this time.

Jim even ran a final dress parade before we opened for business this morning. Good job too. Three guys had pens in full view in their breast pockets – sign of a clerk, not a professional sales executive! Two chaps and one of the girls were sporting brand new shoes. Bet their feet will be killing them by lunchtime.

Fred and Arnold laughed when I told them about my thick wool socks and talcum powder. Let's see who's laughing by mid-week.

First wooden spoon award went to Dave, who at 11.23 precisely sat on one of the visitors' chairs. Harry went into a trance or something at 12.16 and we caught him in a classic prison guard stance, feet ten centimetres over the front edge of the stand, arms folded, 'ready to repel boarders' expression on his face. We pulled his leg unmercifully and he kept saying he didn't know he was doing it. Just shows how easy it is to lose concentration. Those two-hour duty rotas are a winner. We must be working at 95 per cent efficiency. But this is only the first morning.

Our lapel badges are winners, too. They each have our name, the Company's name and a question in letters large enough to be seen about two metres away – 'How can I help you?'

No one believed at the briefing that the question would break the ice with the visitors to our stand the way it is doing. A good 70 per cent are reading the badge, thinking about the question it puts into their minds, and start talking to us before we start talking to them. Great! The addition of that first word, 'How' is helping us avoid that horribly easy-to-fall-into trap of saying to a visitor, 'Can I help you?' I well remember at our last exhibition how many visitors replied -'No thanks. Just looking!'

SALES ENQUIRY		Seen By ....
Name of firm		Date ...././.........././.........
Address		
Business	☎	
Person(s)	Position	
Interested in	Department	
	Quotation/Action Required:-	
Information or Literature Required		
Literature Supplied		
Mailing List Add:	Delete:	

Our exhibition enquiry forms are much better than last time. For the previous exhibition we used a standard form, available from any business stationers. This time, we've designed our own, to make sure we gather precisely the information we need to meet our three main objectives and to cut down writing to a minimum.

The discipline/training/security system seems very good, too. A few members of the stand manning team couldn't understand why Jim Thomson is insisting on all enquiry forms filled in with a visitor being given to him personally at 1.00pm and at close of business each day. The first lot have just been collected, because few of us thought this system could be made to work. So Jim's just given us a short sharp lecture on the reasons behind the system, and warned us that if anyone doesn't deliver tonight and from then on at the designated times, he/she goes home.

Exhibition... Date		
Seen by		
Company		
Address		
....		
Telephone no.		
Contact 1..		
Contact 2		
Type of industry		
┌─ACTION ─		
Standard letter	yes	no
Visit A.S.A.P.	yes	no
Visit by appointment	yes	no
Remarks...		
....		
....		
....		
Mailing list	yes	no
ENQUIRY GRADE		

'You don't even hang on to enquiries for your own territories,' Jim said. 'I need to count, analyse and examine every single one. The more people who carry enquiries around, the greater the danger of losing a few, or having them snatched. Don't underestimate our competitors. The enquiry form that goes missing might be the one that leads to the biggest order we've ever had.

'I'm not only Stand Manager, I'm also head of security. It's my job

SMT-PULLMAX
EXHIBITION Enquiry

Products of interest   Metal Cutting   Metal Forming

Notes on specific details

General information

Budget Price

Quotation

Time Studies

Demonstration

Metal Cutting	Metal Forming
☐ ST 10-220	☐ P31-CNC220
☐ ST 14-220	☐ Pullmax Universal
☐ ST 20-220	☐ Pullmax Beveller X91
☐ VHF/3/3U/3UBS	☐ Pullmax Ring Roller 731
☐ Unidrill 1000	☐ Kumla Rolls PV7H
	☐ Ursviken Press Brakes
	☐ Ursviken Guillotine
	☐ Vikstroms BW300
	☐ Wikstromms BW225/4DV

Literature taken at EXHIBITION stand

☐ General Catalogue m/c   ☐ General Catalogue m/f

Reason for interest

☐ Expanding production   ☐ Seeking to reduce labour force

☐ Replacing existing plant   OTHER

Name.. Position ....

Company..

Address...

....

Telephone Number .... Extension ....

Fax Number.. Email ....

Best Time For Sales Engineer To Call...

to guard these enquiries with my life. They go with me when I leave each night and are locked in the hotel safe. That way, if we get raided at 5.57pm on the last day (everybody laughed at the thought) we only lose one day's enquiries.

'And there's another reason. I want every one of you to bring in the maximum number of good enquiries. So twice each day I'm going to be analysing the forms to see who's performing and who's not. Over the week, I've got eight or nine opportunities to improve anyone's performance – or to replace a real dead-head, if we've got one, with someone who *will* perform. Don't forget the competitions.'

We've accepted the logic and the common sense. But I figure we'll lose Harry by tomorrow night. His mind's obviously on something else – probably that receptionist over on stand 47B.

D-Day Plus 1

Oops! First blunder. What with the euphoria of the first day, we forgot to tidy up last thing last night and get ready for this morning. Sneaky Jim got here half an hour earlier than anyone else – deliberately, I'm sure – and was doing a prison guard stance imitation at us when we arrived. 'What would have happened if there'd been a rail strike or you'd had a puncture and been late?' he hit us with. 'What would visitors have thought of the mess our stand was in when I got here this morning? We don't take the risk.'

Then he lined us up and checked our trouser creases. Seven pairs of trousers failed the test. But it was all done in the right spirit. Again, we all knew what the rules were for making sure we maximized the return on the exhibition investment.

Today the 'SOLD' notices are coming out. We decided it was too early on the first day. This is part of our plan to demoralize our competitors. Everyone has been briefed to wax enthusiastic when talking to competitors and other stand staff and to use words like 'Great' and 'Fantastic' and 'Incredible business we're doing' when questioned.

'SOLD' is the best-selling word in selling

Our 'SOLD' notices hang on the products on our stand. One of our competitions is to aim to sell every product on the stand every day.

More bottles of champagne for the person who sells most each day, *and* for the person who sells the most things across the whole product range, including things not being exhibited.

But the 'SOLD' notices are not directly connected with the competition. When a product has been sold, okay, a 'SOLD' notice is hung on it, but the main plan is to show our competitors that we are selling *all* our products every day (whether or not). They know about our competition; we told them! So every time they look at our stand, they see us doing the great business we're telling them we're doing.

And the laughter they hear they take as the laughter of success.

The visitors see and hear our success, too. And everyone likes to back a winner. So we *do* do great business.

Every morning, the 'SOLD' notices will come off and we'll begin again. By close of business each day, every product on our stand will have a notice hanging on it.

We've other notices, too. Our new products each have a big sign

130

'NEW' above them. The word 'NEW' is the second most powerful buying motivator in the English language, and you can tell that it is effective on an exhibition stand by the crowds of visitors who keep flocking around our 'NEW' products.

D-Day Plus 2

Today we begin our Competitive Tactics plan. I reckon Industrial Espionage is a more accurate term, but the boss wants to keep things strictly legal.

Volunteers were requested for this activity, because it means working pretty hard during the off-duty, two-hour periods and doing a quick change act, out of uniform, into civvies and back again.

Everyone volunteered. No one wanted to miss having a crack at our competitors in this way.

We've been given a checklist of things to do, things to collect, paperwork to acquire. Nowhere on the checklist does it say anything about making the competitor's enquiry and order forms disappear if we see them lying around, but everyone is clear what to do, nevertheless.

Back on our stand, Jim and his 'security force' are going to make sure that we do it to our competitors but they don't do it to us. A couple of the guys are planning to try to steal a few things from our own stand just to test our security. You should see their disguises!

Competitive Tactics Checklist

Make the most of your opportunities.

1. Personal Activities
   Interviews
   Watch their stand
   Attend their lectures
   Tell them how well you are doing

2. Printed Matter
   Collect:
   > sales/technical literature
   > service literature
   > performance information
   > price lists
   > publicity material/company reports

3. Materials
   Obtain:
   > Samples
   > Products
   > Components
   > Other

4. Attend (or take part in):
   tests
   demonstrations

Tonight, back at the hotel, we're getting together to pool our spy achievements and to plan tactics for tomorrow. Bet no one misses that meeting.

D-Day Plus 3

A guy came on the stand this morning with a camera and flashgun, looking official. He was just about to take a picture of our latest and greatest new product when Jim pounced on him and asked him for his ID. It turned out he was a publicity assistant from one of our competitors.

Another lecture from Jim. 'Don't take anyone at face value. Ask for verification – a business card will do. If they've gone to the trouble to get bogus business cards printed, you're not likely to stop them anyway. No one's allowed to take photographs other than the official photographer appointed by the Exhibition Organizer. Remember that.'

At 4.12pm this afternoon Jim made a lightning swoop! We didn't realize we'd been getting slack. We were all still brim-full of enthusiasm. Best exhibition we've ever had, for business, for not getting bored, for fun. Two days to go and we're already over our main target for orders, appointments and names and addresses logged.

Jim found four full ashtrays, three empty glasses, one item of 'left luggage', one raincoat draped over a visitor's chair, two samples lying on the floor instead of in their show case, three duff spotlight bulbs, one displaced polystyrene letter and a portable radio.

As we were already above targets, Jim let us off. But now we're clearing up ready for next morning three times each day.

Ah well, it's all worth it. Think of all that commission we'll be earning in the months to come – all those enquiries we've got to follow up – and that party on Friday night.

'We want the maximum number of customers
beating a path to our door
and begging us to sell them more.

'How? By being nice to our customers,
by being happy, by never putting them down
or making them feel small -
and by using one or two little USPs
I'm going to tell you about.'

Chapter 6

How to Win in Retailing

The rules for winning in Retailing haven't changed in 50 years:

- Rule 1 – get the maximum number of people to walk into your place of business.
- Rule 2 – sell them the maximum amount of goods while they're with you.
- Rule 3 – give them the kind of attention and service that will make them come back for more on a regular basis.

Rules 1 and 3 apply to winning against your competitors down the road or round the corner. Rule 2 applies to the profit you make from your Retailing. The more profit, the more resources you can allocate to achieving 1 and 3.

In this chapter, I'm concentrating on some specific things you can do to increase your USP, unique selling point, and gain an edge – to be better and look better in the eyes of your customers. But first, it is important that we establish what your customers are after.

Retailing is essentially a very simple business. The customers buy from you for only six primary reasons:

1. to save money
2. to maximize usefulness
3. to enhance personal appearance
4. to enhance prestige
6. to enhance comfort
6. because you are convenient.

Okay, if you are in a specialist business, you may have a different reason; for example, if you are an optician, the primary reason for buying would be to see clearly, but enhancing personal appearance might often be more compelling.

If you sold home gymnasiums, the primary reason for buying might be to keep or to get fit, but secondary reasons might be prestige, comfort and (for the track suit and running shoes) again personal appearance.

I am spelling this out because it is incredible how many salespeople in retail stores have obviously never bothered even to think about *why* their customers might want to buy. Nowhere in Selling is product orientation (features not benefits) more rampant than in the retail sector – probably because of an abject lack of training.

If you understand the customer's buying motivation, you're 60 per cent of the way towards a successful sale. You'll know which questions to ask; which benefits of your merchandise to stress; which items to demonstrate or to suggest the customer tries on. You'll also know how best to entice more people into your place of business.

Price Cutting

We are all very familiar with the multi-coloured fluorescent posters that decorate 80 per cent of the retailer's window, advertising 'massive reductions' or 'everything reduced' or '50% off'. Many retailers set out simply to sell on the basis of lowest price, undercutting their competitors, but also undercutting their own profit margins. A classic case of 'Price Fright'. No future!

The astute retailer advertises price cuts only on selected lines; goods of universal appeal or need and goods for which the retailer can negotiate very special terms from the suppliers, either independently or in conjunction with a group of other retailers in different areas. All other goods sold are at the normal prices. Thus, more people are attracted into the place of business by the advertising; they buy the cut-price merchandise and, while they are there, they also buy a number of other things. That's the key Convenience reason playing its part.

Strategically placed point-of-sale displays, adjacent to the cut-price items and also the cash till, can add value to every customer's order. Supermarkets lead the field in exploiting this.

Coffee Service

The higher-class tailors and dress shops sometimes provide an all-day coffee service and a sitting down area. If this is used in conjunction with the browsing sign (see overleaf), the psychological obligation to buy is quadrupled.

But the coffee must be offered as soon as the prospective customer walks into the store. No strings.

'Good morning, Sir, Madam. Terrible day for shopping; will it ever stop raining? We've just put some fresh coffee on, would you and your wife like a cup? How do you like it? Have a look round while I organize things.'

Just as in Flo Wright's Saturday car park technique and at the Hanover Fair café exhibition stand – the coffee is far too hot to drink. So the retailer has the prospective customers comfortably locked in for at least 10 minutes. Worth another 20 per cent on average order value!

Far more retailers could use this technique to beat their competitors and win more business.

The biggest problem is stopping the salespeople drinking all the coffee!

Invite Browsers

Especially for furniture, carpets, hi-fi, and domestic appliances, a professionally painted sign outside the store, on the pavement, works wonders.

The browser browses, but because of the sign inviting him/her into the store just to browse, there is a slight subconscious feeling of obligation, which the retailer can use to break down the normal mental barriers in the prospective customer's mind and to start selling. 'Hello. Have you been in here before?' as a starter, wins 16% more sales than, 'Can I help you?' say the retail researchers.

But don't police the browsers. Don't follow them everywhere. Let them browse properly, once you've told them where you'll be if they want to ask any questions.

Smiles

In retailing, smile is a total concept. You need to be happy every minute of the selling day. And that's hard.

Have a series of prominent posters positioned under every one of your counters and on the back of the staff room door. Have miniatures on every cash till. Run a penalty points competition with a wooden spoon prize for the 'Dismal Jane or Jimmy of the Day'. No one will want to win that one!

Make It EASY To Pay

My wife and I were shopping in Beverley Hills, California. She needed some make-up. We found what she needed with no trouble, the sales girl was very helpful and very good.

Then we tried to pay for what we'd bought. It was only a few dollars, so I offered *cash*.

'Oh. Don't you have a charge account with us?' the sales girl asked.

'No, we're visitors from England,' I replied.

'Ah. Do you have a credit card, then?'

'I do, but I'd prefer to pay cash,' I said happily, totally ignoring the financial revolution that had been taking place around me for the past 30 years.

The sales girl had been trained not to argue with the customer. She took the offered money, asked us to sit down for a few minutes and disappeared.

After 20 minutes she re-appeared, very apologetic, very red, with my change and receipt, explaining the reason for the long wait. I won't bore you with the details – suffice it to say that the store had absolutely no system for handling customers who wanted to pay with actual money.

Pardon the old joke, but in Beverley Hills, money is most certainly the poor person's credit card.

The reason I'm telling you this story is to illustrate the Achilles heel of retailing. It is getting steadily, remorselessly, increasingly more difficult to pay for the goods you've decided to buy.

Even Marks & Spencer haven't cracked this problem, although they've cracked just about every other problem in their kind of retailing. You still have to queue to pay all too often.

When the customer has chosen the goods and is ready to pay for them, *speed* is critically important. Even customers who have taken about an hour to make up their minds expect to be out of the store in a flash once the big decision has been taken. It's a state of mind. If you hold up the paying process, the goods will often go back on the shelves, the customer will stalk out of your place of business in high dudgeon, never, never come back and will tell lots of other people about your abject inefficiency. Unjust it might well be. An isolated case it may well be. You've still lost a customer and a few potential customers.

Petrol retailers know that they have to complete the buying transaction in less than 30 seconds. Any product that takes longer, you won't see in a forecourt shop.

For credit card payments where you've got to telephone for a code number, do the telephoning in full view of the customer, not in some back room. If the customer can see what you're doing, patience will be extended. But in today's retailing, this is still madness. You need the latest credit card automatic electronic system. Invest.

The New Recruits

Retailing is full of incompetent salespeople, thousands of them. A large proportion of them are recent school leavers. They are incompetent only because they have received absolutely no training in how to do their new job – the Selling bit especially. A new recruit is dropped in at the deep end and expected to cope with an incredibly difficult and complex series of tasks. Is it any wonder, therefore, that a high proportion of new recruits don't make it, and while they're suffering, kill quite a few good customers into the bargain?

Every customer is an Alsatian at heart, Walk into a retail store and find yourself up against a new, untrained recruit. How do you react to what you see as incompetence? Grrr! Every time. Frustration, annoyance, even rudeness. It's instinctive. You walked into that store expecting to be looked after, pampered, wooed into parting with your money. Anything less and your hackles go up.

It's the biggest universal problem. Profit margins in Retailing are so low that more training is next to impossible. New recruits are necessary because of the high turnover of sales staff. The new recruits keep killing the customers. Business keeps going down hill.

I have a simple solution to this universal problem. A lapel badge for the new recruits. It says, *'I'm new but I'm trying'*. It's large enough to be read at ten paces. Any new recruit who refuses to wear it has too big an *ego* for retailing and is out of a job!

The potential Alsatian customer gets within eyeshot of the new recruit's lapel badge, reads it automatically and immediately understands. A beaming smile greets the new recruit, who smiles back. Great business is done. Great confidence is built for that new recruit, who graduates to senior sales assistant and maximum commission well inside three months.

Those first-time customers come back a week later and say to the new recruit, 'How are you doing?'

Everyone wins. The new recruit is a competent, confident salesperson, turnover of sales staff falls dramatically, turnover of sales rises dramatically, number of regular customers increases dramatically, competitors wonder what the hell's gone wrong.

And all it took was a lapel badge. At current prices – 20p each.

Returns Anywhere

A while ago I mentioned Marks & Spencer, Britain's top chain on quality, reliability, value for money, and a few things more. But a lot of years of hard work have been put in to make M & S Number One in its field. One of M & S's best USPs is that if something doesn't fit, or you change your mind, or the colour doesn't match the coat you had at home, as long as the item is undamaged and unworn, you can take it back to *any* M & S store and exchange it or get your money back. No questions. No delays.

What a lesson this is to many retailers who don't appear even to have familiarized themselves with the basic statutory rights of the customer under the Sale of Goods Act and a few other more recent pieces of Legislation. They fight tooth and nail to avoid accepting anything back and especially giving a refund. And very quickly indeed, the word gets round the area, and within weeks the 'Shop To Let' and 'Closing Down Sale' notices go up.

You Need Regulars

Every retailer needs as many *regular* customers as possible. Work hard to add to them. Regular customers bring in your steady bread-and-butter turnover. They recommend your store to other people.

Remember their names. Greet them by name when they call. Offer them monthly account and delivery facilities. When you've learnt their interests, write to them from time to time when you have something that you feel is right for them.

The cost of selling to regular customers is less than to passing trade, because it's quicker and their needs are known, and because that all-important confidence in you, your name and your merchandise has already been built up.

But don't take your regulars for granted. Losing one is 100 times worse for your business than losing a passing-trade customer.

Position, Position, Position

Just as for an exhibition stand, the Hilton Rule applies universally to Retailing. If your store is in the right position, you'll do well. If it is not, you'll spend an arm and a leg on advertising and still maybe not attract as many customers into your place of business as the competitor who has picked the best position.

But what *is* the best position? It depends on the business, of course. I used to buy my greengrocery from a tiny little lock-up shop in Royal Leamington Spa, sandwiched between the rear entrances of Woolworth's and Marks & Spencer's stores.

Opposite the tiny lock-up shop is the town's largest furniture store and a car park.

That's position. The tiny lock-up shop is always full of customers. It has more turnover than any two other greengrocers in the town. It delivers for its regulars. It takes telephone orders and its sales girls bring the boxes out to your car, which can park for a few minutes to load directly outside the shop. Its pavement displays are mouthwatering.

Its passing trade is tremendous, because greengroceries are mainly impulse buys. So many of the customers of Woolworth's, M&S and the furniture store, and the people who use the car park, buy from that little lock-up shop because it is so convenient.

Summing Up

This book is full of real-life examples of how to find NEW customers. Chances are, you'll find half a dozen that you can take straight out of the pages and use. If you're in a VERY specialist business, not covered by anything, I hope these examples help you open your mind and start developing your own differences – ways to be your own USP in your unique business.

That's the key thing to remember ...

YOU

ARE

UNIQUE

Index

Advances of your competitors, 62
Advertisements, 19
Annual Reports, 21

Bad news travels fast, 62
Being an entrepreneur, 33
  better, 80
Beating the bribers, 97
Being faster, 94
  honest, 96
  thorough, 87
Big Mouth!, 102
Browsers, 137
Business cards, 47
'By appointment only', 45

Car spotting, 34
Carrots, 16
Checklists, 87
Cocktail party prospecting, 33
Coffee service, 137
Cold canvassing, 43
  by telephone, 56
Competitive salespersonship, 78
Complaints, 64
Council Planning Registers, 23
Customer's shoes, 52

Detectives, 16
Dishonest buyer, 99
Domestic selling, 84

Early risers, 36
End of call questions, 25
Exhibitions, 105
Exhibition budget, 109

Files, 73
Finding new customers, 15
Five card trick, 28
Focusing the mind, 82

Gifts, 96
Gold medals, 39

'Hilton' Rule, 111
Hospitality, 115

Internal promotions, 21

Jekyll-and-Hyde technique, 55

Key stages, 91

Local job advertisements, 19

Making it easy to pay, 139
Minders, 38
Models, 114
Motivation, 66

Negative thinking, 80
New recruits, 140

Ostrich complex, 65

PLC Annual Reports, 21
Plot and counter-plot, 100
Position, 143
Price cutting, 136
Profile of a sale, 91
Prospects, 29
Purchasing cycle plan, 75

Reasons to change, 94
Referrals, 25
Regular customers, 143
Retailing, 135
Returns, 142
Rumours, 68

Searching for names, 30
Second oldest profession, 11
Second source, 97
Selling the difference, 67
Short-circuiting the politics, 78
Smiles, 138

Staffing the stand, 120
Stands at exhibitions, 112
Star prize, 38
Survey checklists, 92

Taking advantage, 70
Telephones, 114
Titles, 51
Trade exhibitions, 105
Two kinds of people, 85

Ultimate referral technique, 28
Unique selling point, 135
Very poor odds, 66

Why are you exhibiting?, 107
Winning in retailing 135
  more business, 73

Yorick from Warwick, 57